At the grand old age of 77, I have, very reluctantly, decided to retire after a 61-year working life. But I still refuse to be inactive! The only 'tool' of my working life has been the pen. Reading and writing have, therefore, been a principle occupational activity for many years. So, I have decided to try to become an author. I left school in 1956, aged 15, with no certificates whatsoever. I started work as an 'office boy' (junior clerk). In 2017, I completed my last job as town clerk for a council in the East Midlands. I have been a manager of a large school's resources centre for 15 years; admin officer in a university's careers' advisory service for 12 years; a county council redeployment officer for five years; and numerous other employment posts, both full time and part time. I have a post-graduate diploma in management and thoroughly enjoy researching matters, particularly, but not restricted to, occupational employment matters.

I am a family man and remain a lifetime supporter of Nottingham Forest Football Club (This has proved to be quite a challenging exercise during the last few years and I count this as both an attribute and achievement!).

Malcolm F Plumb

THE OPPORTUNITY OF UNEMPLOYMENT

ROUTE PLAN

AUSTIN MACAULEY PUBLISHERS™

LONDON · CAMBRIDGE · NEW YORK · SHARJAH

A CIP catalogue record for this title is available from the British Library.

ISBN 9781528928304 (Paperback)
ISBN 9781528965422 (ePub e-book)

www.austinmacauley.com

First Published (2020)
Austin Macauley Publishers Ltd
25 Canada Square
Canary Wharf
London
E14 5LQ

Much of my book is based upon over 60 years' occupational experience, working at both junior and executive levels, for a variety of employers in the commercial and public sector, both full time and part time. It is also based upon learning experiences in managerial and organisational roles, and professional management studies.

More recently, I have researched many excellent websites, watched TV documentaries and read a number of relevant and inspirational books, five of which are listed below. I have listened to outstanding pieces of inspirational music, e.g., M People – *"You've got to search for the hero inside yourself,"* which seems to me to sum up a major aspect of dealing with unemployment.

My sincere appreciation and unreserved acknowledgements are extended to all these people, and many more, who have guided my working life over many years in the past.

Who Moved My Cheese?	Dr Spencer Johnson
No Fears, No Excuses	Larry Smith
The Little Book of Thinking Big	Richard Newton
The Secret	Rhonda Byrne
Psychology of Success	Alison and David Price

Table of Contents

Introduction

Government statistics currently claim (2018) that about 1.5 million are registered as unemployed in the U.K. Others argue that the true figure is much higher. Above this are people who are unemployed but are not registered as such for one reason or another (e.g. disability). Whatever the true figure is, there is yet another aspect to this situation. The 'turnover' of people having to change their jobs is very much higher these days because of changing technology, market forces, environmental considerations and government policies. And these changes are accelerating with the growth of IT. The belief of 'having a job for life' in any type of organisation is, of course, long since gone. A recent report estimated that up to 800 million global workers will lose their jobs by 2030 and be replaced by robotic automation. This estimate followed a study of 46 ('developed') countries and some 800 occupations. Hardest hit will be machine operators and food workers. About 35% of current jobs in the UK are at a high risk of computerisation over the next 20 years. Websites can be used to check the current % risk of your own occupation being affected. Not all jobs can be automated, of course, whatever 'Spock' from 'Star Trek' might think! However, developmental change, **itself**, produces many new forms of occupations. Dealing with unemployment/redeployment is still (sadly) a matter of interest to <u>all</u>. Even if you feel you are not at risk, a 'fall back plan' is prudent for <u>everyone</u> to have.

<u>Unemployment</u> actually really does represent an **opportunity** for a person to improve or at least protect their whole lifestyle, although many would not believe this, certainly at the offset. <u>This book sets out to justify that assertion</u>. No sensible person could deny the many traumatic

feelings that unemployment brings, the personal stress, the financial worries, and the disruption to life styles and the effects upon families, friends and even whole communities. No attempt will be made to ignore these experiences, and the work needed of having, suddenly, to rebuild a major part of your life. Indeed, it is essential for you and I to identify, and openly examine these matters in some detail and then, to come to terms with them, even if the threat does not exist at present. Not many people can be expected to stride positively and confidently into a recruiting interview, having perhaps earlier received a demand for mortgage arrears.

The aim of this particular book then, is to deal with **THE WHOLE** experience of unemployment, as a springboard to a happier and more successful life. To use a 'disaster' as an 'opportunity route', in order to acquire increased happiness and success. The book is mainly aimed at people in what I call the 'middle occupational employment' fields, the 'average' (if you will) job. Highly professional, executive, scientific occupations may find less help in the book. All though some parts might still be useful for such highly specialised occupations, which have become redundant, through technical advances. This 'attempt to help' publication might, therefore, prove to be a useful reference, to keep for the immediate future, at least by most people, to some extent or other.

It is written in three sections. Firstly, it aims to tackle the very first dangers and problems that unemployment can cause you as a person. The second (larger) section deals with the route plan you can take, to help convert a 'disaster' into a change that will enrich your whole life or at least preserve your current position. The final (shorter) section provides a number of suggestions to help ensure your new occupation is a happier, more rewarding and fulfilling experience for yourself and your family and friends.

We will examine the WHOLE unemployment problem openly and understand the important characteristics of the experience, and one 'ROUTE' you can travel in order to make the change from being a VICTIM of unemployment, to being a SUCCEEDER in new employment, whatever the nature of that new occupation/employment is.

As one friend of mine pointed out some time ago:

"Unemployment actually turned out to be a blessing in disguise. Once I had picked myself up and reorganised my life, I obtained a much more secure, rewarding and fulfilling career and a far happier life generally."

Section One

The Unemployment Experience

Unemployment is affecting many more people than government statistics claim. The principle culprit is the growing speed with which changes are occurring within our society, from a technology perspective, from 'market forces', increased competition, weakening economies and public policy (government actions). 'Change' is, nowadays, INEVITABLE, for everyone. Anyone who has already lived through the trauma of unemployment will appreciate that the problems very often start well before official notifications of termination of employment.

Let us consider, as a first step, three main stages of becoming unemployed. These being threatened unemployment, the actual event of becoming unemployed, and finally the experience of being 'long-term unemployed'.

Threatened Unemployment

Threatened unemployment, possibly because of the uncertainty involved, can be as stressful an experience as the actual event. Most people have a fair idea about how unemployment occurs and, to some extent, it does concern you (as an individual) to know how, in your particular case, this has occurred , how it might happen in the future, and to have some idea as to what you can do about it. Of course, unemployment can happen through voluntary resignation, or 'sacking', and you will know all the circumstances leading up to your own case. Similarly, ill health can have made it impossible for you to carry out a particular kind of work. Uncertainty arises where redundancy is threatened or rumoured and this can be because of things like market forces (e.g. what is being sold and what is no longer being sold), changed political policies or technological development. These events can make-or-break careers, jobs and employment opportunities

Once a 'corporate' decision has been taken in the boardroom or a public body, to 'rationalise', 'economise', 'automate', 'computerise' or 'restructure', the question comes up: 'who gets the chop?' In the past, the trade unions have been able, under past legislation, (to their credit!) to influence matters and whatever the media or politicians may say, have carried out many worthy struggles to protect worker's rights from policies wholly designed to make the rich richer and the poor poorer! Current legislation now restricts that power, and market and political forces, have the major say. You, therefore, need to start taking the right kind of action <u>for yourself</u> at the earliest opportunity BEFORE (if possible) the actual unemployment event takes place.

So, let's get into the habit from the very beginning of taking a PRO-ACTIVE stance rather than a RE-ACTIVE one. Assume that your board of management has announced that over the next six to twelve months, 40% of the work force will have to 'go' in order to cut costs and avoid bankruptcy. What do you do immediately? Here are a few 'Do's and Don'ts':

DON'T waste your time considering rumours and other people's speculations. Search only for the <u>verifiable</u> truths and facts.

DON'T get involved in heated arguments with others over why the situation is occurring.

DON'T waste your time looking for someone to blame.

DON'T drop your working standards (time keeping, work quality etc.).

DON'T isolate yourself from others.

DO carry out your own evaluation on your own chances of being selected for redundancy (see notes below).

DO start to build up a career history for yourself (advice given later).

DO carry out a detailed review of your personal income and expenditure (advice given later).

DO talk openly to your family and close (trusted) friends about the developing situation.

Do set up for yourself, a <u>search mission</u> for alternative employment (suggested action given later).

Redundancy' is a term which has been defined by the law (Employment Act 1996), and all employers must take note of this legislation. The two most significant definitions are; 'The employer has ceased to carry on the business' and/or 'The employer has ceased to need a particular work type/occupation.' However, the law does not specifically cover <u>all</u> causes of redundancy. For example, one major corporation may 'buy out' a 'competing' corporation and then 're-structure' specifically to reduce costs and to economise.

Unless the threatened unemployment affects <u>everyone</u> within the organisation, (e.g. bankruptcy, closure of a factory etc.), the employer has a legal duty to consider alternative measures to redundancy. The most important ones, to you, are:

- 'Internal redeployment'. Vacancies are created anyway by 'natural wastage' through people moving onto other jobs, retirements, or by new internal opportunities. Employees at risk should be given first preference in filling these jobs.
- The employer should consider alternative action to redundancy, e.g. short-time working, voluntary scheme of redundancy or early retirement, short-term 'layoffs'.
- The employer should carry out a process of consultation with the trade unions or employee's associations upon the changing position.
- The employer should establish fair rules upon <u>how</u> people are to be selected for redundancy (sometimes called the 'selection criteria').
- The circumstances of any offer of alternative employment to employees 'at risk', must be specified

to, and accepted by, the employee concerned. If an offer of alternative employment is made and is unreasonably refused by the employee, this can affect rights to redundancy payments.

It is more likely that these actions are taken by larger organisations with a large workforce, than for those with fewer employees. For example, a 'good' employer may even give, as an additional form of assistance to employees being 'laid off', by helping them to obtain <u>outside jobs</u> (called 'outplacement') with another employer. Nevertheless, these are still issues to discuss with management.

In assessing your own chances of being made redundant, consider the following.

- What is your <u>length of service</u> with the employer compared to others? ('Last in, first out' is one rule but other aspects can be applied). On this point about length of service, bear in mind that the minimum period of continuous employment for the purpose of redundancy claims is two years.
- <u>How essential is your own work</u>/contribution? If it was not done would the whole operation stop? Could it be easily done by others or by that dreaded word, 'IT'.
- Could your job be <u>'automated'</u>?
- How good is <u>your attendance/absence record</u>?
- Is <u>your work experience, qualification, and training</u> satisfactory for this work, better than others, or worse?
- Have you been involved in any <u>previous disciplinary action</u> or 'difficulties' with management?

Answering these questions for yourself will give you an indication of your chances of selection for redundancy, but do be realistic. If a medical problem with your spine has caused you to take a number of periods off work during the last year, this <u>can</u> be taken into consideration by management.

Conversely, if you are the only employee who can operate complicated, essential machinery or plant, points can be scored in your favour unless, of course, your work can be 'robotised'. As you consider each of these aspects, take into account the likely extent of redundancies. Is it 50% of the workforce or 5%? Obviously, your chances of avoiding redundancy are better in the second case. Finally, it has to be admitted that 'personality' issues can (alas) creep into the process of deciding 'who goes and who stays'. Do not allow this possibility to assume excessive importance, but answer for yourself the following additional questions:

- Have you had any supervisors, managers, or directors during the past two years with whom you have experienced either working or personal difficulties? How much influence do they have in the decision-making process?
- What is my personal standing (popularity) amongst my immediate working group?

Once you have completed this task, you will have a more realistic view of your chances of being selected for, or, escaping, redundancy. You may well also have created your case for arguing that you should be retained in employment, should you be given such an opportunity. Finally, you will also be able to formulate some preliminary ideas for future plans. Do you want to stay with your current employer and occupation type, given the opportunity to do so? Is your work experience limited? Are you a 'team player' or do you work better on your own? Finally, keep a note of any work done which you did well and enjoyed, particularly where you made things 'better'. Have you done something which could reasonably be described as creating a permanent working benefit to your employer, or others for the future? This exercise may well become useful as you travel along 'the route'. Conversely, what work did you not like? Or you think you may have 'failed' in

As the prospective of unemployment threatens, the main question begins to emerge: 'can I get another job?' Initially, many people are inclined to take a negative response and conclude that re-employment prospects are bleak. Finding alternative employment is not easy for many people, but you can be sure of one thing at least. It will be virtually impossible for someone to get alternative employment, who takes no action to help themselves. Whilst you may not know for certain at this time whether you are to be made redundant, the essential thing is to make as many preparations as you can and as early as possible. It has been proved by past research that the earlier you start work to obtain alternative employment, the better your chances are for success. Whatever the future holds, you are going to need a description of your past life in relation to your work experience, your training, your education/qualifications, the talents you think you have, and details of what you regard as your past achievements. So, begin to collect information about your past and present career and your past jobs in order to help complete future job applications (your 'Curriculum Vitae'). More information is given on this task later in this book.

Actual Unemployment

When *actual unemployment* occurs (formal redundancy notice), it is almost impossible to describe the effects on different people. For some, it is an experience of catastrophic proportions, equal to a bereavement of a loved relative or friend. It can be a crisis in terms of your lifestyle, your financial position, and standard of living, and also, in terms of your self-confidence. For others, it might not cause worry or stress, but even so, they still need to take action to deal with this problem. There are many unpleasant emotions and consequences, and it would be quite wrong for anyone to attempt to suppress or hide these effects. Whether the unemployment experience occurs suddenly (literally in minutes) or after a period of 'warning signs', the sense of shock experienced by the majority of the 'victims' is rarely mild. Whilst it is true that a few people—outwardly at least—seem to cope with the experience better than most, unemployment universally, is an unpleasant experience for anyone to deal with.

Managing this problem begins with understanding its detailed characteristics and identifying alternative courses of action or remedial solutions. It is essential for anyone who experiences sudden unemployment to recognise from the very outset that they need the support and fellowship of others. This is not a time to detach/isolate yourself socially as we will see shortly. The most common first experience at this stage can be summed up in one word—'Anxiety'. So, let us consider, in simple terms, the nature of this problem and how we might tackle it.

It is claimed that anxiety, shock or sudden bad news causes many people to experience certain known stages. Approximately these are:

1. **Disbelief;** non-acceptance, rejection of the news/event
2. **Realisation;** acceptance of the event, followed by anxiety
3. **Depression**; grief, sorrow, stress.
4. **Detachment**; isolation.

5. **Final acceptance**; of the event
6. **Coming to terms;** with the event.

For the sake of simplicity, we might consider three levels of the <u>extent</u> of stress and anxiety.

A **mild** level of stress involving perhaps slight tenseness and a reduction in concentration can be handled in the first instance by you. Improving your diet, keeping busy with meaningful work, taking up more physical exercise can be effective remedies. If you become <u>physically</u> tired, your body automatically relaxes after the exercise. At the same time, <u>your mind</u> also seems to relax and the stress level is reduced. At this stage, try not to resort to drugs. This may be appropriate for the next level.

A **medium** level of stress may well involve sleeplessness, increased irritability and unexplained tiredness. The options suggested above can be tried, but at this level, you also need the support and involvement of family and friends. You must communicate with people. At any level of stress, isolation from others must be avoided at all costs. Introduce into your routine periods of relaxation and if this does not work, time to discuss the situation with your GP.

A **high** level of stress MUST be taken seriously. See your GP, ideally with a member of your close family. An 'extra pair of ears' at this appointment can be very useful. Relate to your doctor all the symptoms you are experiencing, explain the current position of your employment situation and give details of how you have tried to deal with the situation yourself. Then take their advice and agree to a 'review' appointment.

You must try to preserve and develop your own self-esteem and self-confidence. One of the physical consequences of someone suffering from stress is that they can become untidy, overweight and sometimes inarticulate. This is certainly not the state of affairs which you want when meeting potential future employers. Be aware of this and maintain your own personal standards.

Remember anxiety/stress is a natural response to a major change in one's life. It is normally temporary. It must be recognised and attended to, in order to achieve your main objective; acquiring a better career and life!

Unemployment **is** a crisis and it is actually at its most damaging form when it creates depression and affects your self-confidence. It makes you feel that you have, somehow, become a lesser person. **Nothing could be further from the truth**. Despite the fact that it is very difficult for unemployed people to maintain their own self-confidence level through this period, the fact is they are exactly the same person as before with all their strength's, talents and attributes which they held previously. The frustrations, fears and disappointments that now cause much pain are also character and personality building experiences. It is the JOB which has disappeared. It is the ORGANISATION which has failed. **You have not**. Was it just your own actions which brought about the unemployment scenario? In the vast majority of cases, it was, most certainly, not.

The conventional (pessimistic) view is that unemployment is growing, many firms are closing down and cutting back and the only jobs which are available are either low wage positions, commission only jobs or work of a highly technical nature. THIS VIEW IS UTTERLY WRONG! It is a view often expressed by the press and media. There is a well-known saying which I want you to remember; **'Disaster scenarios sell newspapers' (but rarely give the whole accurate story).** At the time of writing this book, the proposed 'Brexit' change next year is the subject of a wide selection of speculative predictions from the media, political parties and other pressure groups, some of which are quite extraordinary. I, personally, have a lot more faith and confidence in the British Nation and its people to ultimately make the changes needed to create a resounding success story. This means being prepared to adapt, to change, and to identify new opportunities to develop and work on. This is the most important basic philosophy of this book. So, do not allow the 'doom and gloom' brigade to make you forget one essential truth; if 'change' is inevitable, **as it is anyway**, new situations **always** create new opportunities for both you, personally, and for the country as a whole. You only need one single job/occupation for yourself in the changed circumstances. There is always room for one better employee. **YOU!**

It is true that jobs are being lost every single day. In the past, the coal mining industry was one such example (for reasons of cleaner air). But it is also true, that about one million new (and different types) of jobs are being created every year. The employee who takes a greater interest in noting activities and businesses which are 'dying' and those activities which are taking over and/or expanding, is better able to plan their **'route'** to a better life. For instance, there is now little demand for servicing stage coach candle lanterns nowadays (to use a ridiculous example to illustrate the point!). An advanced society like ours is absolutely dependent upon new opportunities being created literally every single day. How else could we possibly keep up to date? The whole concept, for example, of competition, requires that new techniques, new systems, better organisation, lower costs, different skills are needed and are being developed every single day. **Change, itself, therefore, throws up a continuous stream of NEW opportunities**. It also creates, of course, many new problems. But problems themselves can be made to create improvements and new opportunities! The employee who can help solve these problems for an employer gets employed (whatever the press might say). So, let's start at the beginning by recognising everyone has their own strengths, skills, talents and occupational experiences. What is now needed is work on maintaining self-confidence. We will now consider this in greater detail.

Self-Confidence

It is fully understood that **Self-confidence** is bound to be affected for many people by the incidence of unemployment. In a later section, I have given some suggestions upon how to handle your personal life in the intervening period between

25

jobs (e.g. activities and home finances). I have previously mentioned known stages which many people experience in dealing with 'anxiety'. During the first 4 stages, it is tempting to become wholly withdrawn, lethargic and perhaps irritable. Your first steps, therefore, must be to combat this understandable reaction. You must get into the habit of turning a problem into an opportunity. In place of being EMPLOYED, for present, you now have been given, temporarily, **TIME**. Regard this as a valuable new resource for YOU. You must use it!

If it is your intention to remain in the same kind of occupation as in your past, (see later suggestions on this subject), you need to start by taking steps to maintain your occupational knowledge. Visits to the public library, using specialist publications, researching the 'web' will help in this regard. Maintaining contact with past working colleagues, with whom you enjoyed a good working relationship, can be useful in exchanging information upon new opportunities. One of these past contacts might be your previous immediate supervisor, who might be willing to provide a future reference

One thing you must **not** do is to accept any 'negative' attitudes which you may be tempted to have at this time about yourself. Such things as:

'A leopard cannot change its spots.'

'I have to accept the present situation because there is no alternative.'

'Maybe next year more opportunities will arise.'

'My old method of working was OK. Why change it?'

'If your face does not fit, you are going nowhere.'

'I am a nurse and I am not interested in anything else.'

The most important point which you must remember at this time is this:

'Nobody can become a better, more successful person by remaining what they are.'

By dumping whatever negative attitudes held in the past, by being relieved of all the frustrations which you have so far suffered, you have started to change what you were and given yourself a clean sheet with which to make a fresh start. Not convinced? Then consider the following ***real-life*** career changes;

The telephone operator who became a multi-millionaire shipping magnate (Adstotle Onassis).
The sausage maker who became a famous international footballer (Chris Waddle).
The toffee puller (really!) who became an all-time international entertainer (Bob Hope).
The insurance clerk who became a world-famous ice skater (Jayne Torvill).
The art teacher who became a well-respected member of parliament (Mary Whitehouse)

And just recently:

The furniture shop owner, who built the world-wide IKEA network (Ingvar Kamprad).
These are just six examples of literally thousands of other cases. There is no reason why you cannot add your own name to this list. Or at the very least, considerably improve the quality of your whole life by being much more successful in your current occupation or by willing to change to a wholly different one.
In his excellent book, *'Who moved my cheese?'* by Dr Spencer Johnson, in his tale upon the fortunes (and misfortunes) of two imaginary mice and two 'little people', Dr Johnson quoted A J Cronin's following quotation.

"Life is no straight and easy corridor along which
We travel free and unhampered, but
A maze of passages through which we must seek
Our way, lost and confused, now and again checked
In a blind alley
But always, if we have faith, a door will open for us

Not perhaps one that we ourselves would
ever have thought of, but one that
will ultimately prove good for us."

Long-Term Unemployed / Registered Disabled

If you have been **unemployed** for some time, say, a year, you are likely to be under some form of monitoring and reviews whilst you are in receipt of 'job seekers allowances'. You may well have received already, assistance in securing a new job, but have not yet succeeded. As one or two people have commented, this assistance is limited in value, aimed principally at reducing public expenditure costs at any price by simply getting you into <u>any</u> job. Whatever the reason is, you have to accept that if you <u>really</u> want to work in a job you enjoy and receive appropriate pay, you, <u>yourself,</u> have to make real, determined, efforts to meet this aim.

Even if you are **disabled** in some way, this rule, <u>still</u> applies, because <u>every person who has a disability, **retains, other forms of ability.**</u> Can you <u>see,</u> can you <u>hear,</u> can you <u>walk,</u> can you <u>think,</u> can you use your <u>hands</u> still? The answers you give yourself will begin to define work that you **still** can do. I remember a guy I met who was severely disabled with unusable legs, and a severe spinal deformity. He got around on a highly specialised wheel chair, but he had full use of his arms, normal eyesight and an enquiring mind. He got a job as a library assistant, re-shelving books and cataloguing records. He took a correspondence course and his employer provided every assistance to facilitate his studies. After some 2–3 years, he was promoted to librarian, was extremely happy in his work and became an inspiration to everyone who came to know him. The lesson for anyone disabled or long term unemployed is this: **'Think not what you CANNOT do, think more what you CAN do.'**

For those who are 'long-term unemployed' who <u>do</u> have all their faculties, I strongly urge you to start your journey by moving onto to Section Two in this book, 'Redeployment work and action', and, to make a <u>determined</u> effort to go through the work and activities suggested. These include identifying your true occupational interests, experience, talents and skills, followed by a systematic job search, and sending in good quality job applications. If, however, you are **determined** to remain unemployed, then simply, this book will not give you the kind of help you need. And you **do** need help, because whatever your circumstances are, you can still improve the quality of your life by 'working'. **Your** choice!

For registered disabled, who are not severely and permanently mentally impaired, and you are able to see, hear, speak (or otherwise) communicate, think about things reasonably well, you **can** obtain a happier life by the more careful choice of occupation. In addition to the example given to us, by our librarian above, recall the most commendable case of Professor Stephen Hawkins.

Richard Newton's excellent book *The Little Book of Thinking Big* provides more helpful 'habits' of 'thinking big' (and positive). 'Habit 5', in discussing the reality and inevitability of change, he comments, "We all have an instinct to fear change. It is a constant and unavoidable part of our lives." Habit 5 summarises two choices when change occurs, 'accept or resist'. Acceptance says, 'OK, let's work with this.' Another 'habit', Number 3 ('feed your mind'), relates the story of the changes in the lives of Pacific Island Communities by military cargo aircraft activities during World War II. The Islanders saw the benefit that these 'strange' people had, like available food, odd clothing and living styles and the Islanders tried to mimic them as if they were 'Gods'. Their problem was not lack of imagination; it was NOT knowing enough. <u>'Feeding' your brain IS essential</u> (making sure, of course, that you feed in only the facts and <u>verifiable</u> truths). More of this later.

First Considerations

One aspect of unemployment which must be addressed, if we are to look at the whole picture of unemployment, is where the unemployment is the result of 'sacking' for misconduct or disciplinary reasons. If the reasons given by the employer are <u>fully</u> justified, (employees have a right to challenge them if they so wish), the 'sacking' might be (simply) classified into two basic causes. Firstly, dishonesty and/or serious misconduct, and secondly, repeated failure to meet the employees' own responsibilities in the job (e.g. poor performance).

In the first place (i.e. proven dishonesty, serious misconduct), there is simply no advice which can be given, except to greatly improve his/her standard of conduct, honesty and attitude—as a <u>permanent</u> aspect of their personality. I know that (sadly), there are cases—other than the 'success' references given above—where others have achieved success <u>through</u> misconduct, seriously bad behaviour and dishonesty. This factor, however, does not justify anyone following the same lines. Notwithstanding this, it is not intended to offer any further advice in these cases, than that given above that is, '<u>Improve your own standards!</u>'

The second cause of 'sacking', (repeated failure to meet the employer's occupational requirements, disciplinary actions), is, however, fully capable of being dealt with, along perhaps the following lines:

- Obtain from the employer the full and specific details of where the jobs responsibilities have not been met, or the detailed reasons for disciplinary action. How were performances measured and what actions breached the employer's policy on discipline?
- Have you had 'work appraisal' reviews carried out? Were you satisfied with these?
- Have you been given additional training and/or closer supervision to help you deal with the problem?
- Is your attendance record satisfactory? Do you get on with others as a 'team player'?

'Satisfactory working' is, of course, a relative term, measured against some form of yardstick. The easiest example is the salesman, who consistently failed to meet reasonable targets. Another example might be a service engineer who is sacked because other engineers had to complete or correct his work. It is essential for the employee concerned to be completely realistic and honest about these questions, because their future happiness and success at work is strongly dependent upon this. Was the service engineer not only making mistakes in the technical work, but was also a 'loner' working in an organised 'team' workshop, did not accept the authority of his supervisor and was often 'experimenting' with circuits, rather than carrying out essential servicing jobs.

Now, our engineer in this scenario might allow bitterness and anger to rule his actions, be arrogant and continue to believe that he or she is right, or, <u>to accept and use the experience and try to improve their performance and attitude?</u> 'Weaknesses' can be dealt with in a number of different ways, once it has been accepted this is the problem. Retraining for the absence of a technical/professional skills or counselling for 'personality' problems are just two examples. If mistakes <u>have been made</u> in the job, do not ignore them. They are important pointers to improving your work. If our engineer cannot change and improve, despite justified criticism, then the blunt truth might be that they may, simply, be in the <u>wrong job</u>. In a later chapter, we will be examining 'self-analysis', which helps to identify alternative occupations more suitable to people, in a case like this.

Rebuilding Self-Confidence

When a person has a high level of self-confidence, that person is normally successful at work and happy in their personal life. But, a word of caution at this stage; <u>too much self-confidence</u> can lead to a person becoming arrogant and inflexible. A realistic balance between the two extremes should be aimed for. You can, in fact, be outstanding in your work, <u>but you can still learn from others and from your on-</u>

going experiences. Albert Einstein was still learning new truths **after** creating his famous equation.

Clearly, there is a level of self-confidence which is right for you, personally, based on your personality and past experience/knowledge. However, unemployment can and does have an impact. On this route that you are travelling, you need to establish, in your own mind, realistic and positive beliefs about yourself in a number of key areas. So, let's consider this aspect in greater detail. It is important.

As soon as we are born into this life, a continuous stream of information is fed into our minds. As a baby, we learn the importance of the warmth, security and nourishment that our parents provide. Early childhood provides experiences which may well shape a large proportion of how we view ourselves. Attendance at schools will influence our interests, abilities and personality, positively (OR negatively). Your mind is, therefore, constantly storing vast quantities of data, information and experiences. This process goes on continually throughout our lives. Consider, for example, the following incidents:

- Supervised by her mother, a three-year-old girl is playing in a paddling pool. The mother's attention is momentarily distracted at the same time as the child slips and falls underneath the water for a time and is badly frightened by the experience before her mother rescues her.
- A school teacher goes out of her way to compliment a drawing done by a disabled child.
- A young boy asks if he can help his father with some house painting work. Father is in an irritable mood and impatiently dismisses him with the answer, "Don't be silly, you can't do that!"
- A young lady finally catches the eye of a young man she likes, by changing her hair style.

You will immediately appreciate that these kinds of incidents are happening all the time. Some will have a positive impact upon our interests and personality, others will have a negative impact even after the memory of the incident has been lost or stored in our sub conscious mind memory. The important thing to recognise is that everyone's self-confidence level is very much a product of their life experiences, even though they may have become long forgotten. The small child in the first case grows into a young woman, forgets completely the incident in the paddling pool, but is fearful of water and cannot swim. You and I both know that, with a minimum of effect, she can, in fact, learn to swim, but she still believes that she is incapable of doing so. The disabled child grows up equipped with the strong belief in her own artistic and creative talents, long after the incident in the classroom has been 'forgotten'.

Just spend a few moments now to allow this factor to penetrate into your mind. Consider what fears you might have about yourself and the experiences you might have forgotten. I myself always had a fear of foreign languages and anything mathematical. At about 38 years of age, I met an old school friend and we reminisced about our school days. It was during that conversation that I learned that the Maths, French and RI (religious instruction!) teachers had been either transferred to other duties and/or sent for further training.

Your own brain is, (in my view at least), the most magnificent computer on this planet, and, like any other computer, it operates, partially, on the instructions of the 'software programs' that are fed into its memory cells. The young son in the third case cited above may well avoid decorating or similar tasks because he does not particularly enjoys the work and he thinks 'he cannot do it' for some reason which escapes his memory. His brain is merely behaving in accordance with earlier 'learning'.

The important thing about this scenario is that in the same way a computer can be 're-programmed', the subconscious image you have of yourself can also be improved and developed. Those hidden artificial mental barriers can be broken down and replaced with more positive instructions about your abilities and strengths. If you were unhappy, anyway, at work, this is NOT a reflection upon your talents, abilities and attributes. The constituent elements of the job were not in tune with your skills, interests, values, personality and past experiences. Redundancy is NOT a reflection of you as a person. The experience, itself will, in a short period of time, make you a better, wiser and experienced person.

- A 'victim' will remain a victim the longer they do little to help themselves and allow their circumstances to control events.
- A 'survivor' will take positive action to influence events to their own preferences.

The Power of the Human Mind

To try to define the capacity of the human mind is well beyond the capability of myself (and perhaps many other people) at present. It is necessary, however, to dwell on this subject a little while longer. The reason is that before you embark on your journey to a better occupation and life ('the route'), you need to have a healthy belief in your own potential and a reasonable level of self-confidence (not arrogance). As has already been said, the human mind is capable of performing acts of literally miraculous proportions. Human-kind seems to be evolving to a better understanding of this. The good news is that being already equipped with the 'hardware' (the brain), you only need the (mental) 'software' to achieve anything you want.

Consider, for a moment, the mental processes that are occurring whilst—say—you are travelling to work in your car. You know the route so you need little concentration other than driving safely. As you go along, without 'thinking', you are changing gear, accelerating, braking, steering round corners, indicating and keeping an eye on the silly so-and-so who is driving rather too close to your rear. You are receiving information, making decisions, and taking action, every single second. At the same time, you might be listening to a discussion on the car radio or remembering incidents which occurred during last night's football match. You arrive at work with very little recollection of the journey. You would not feel that you had put much effort into the drive that you do every day. Agreed? The journey was uneventful. At the time of writing this book, the incidence of 'driverless cars and trains' is being slowly 'trialled' and actually implemented. The difference is, it is being done by computer technology of a very, very, advanced level. But you have been doing this 'without thinking' for a long time, without much effort!

In my own view, therefore, the most important part of your whole body is located in your head! The human brain is a <u>magnificent facility.</u> Many highly respected, famous, and knowledgeable people both in the past and present believe (and demonstrate by their own example) that the normal human brain **is** actually capable of much greater abilities and achievements, that humankind has <u>yet</u> to discover. Consider again, the example created for us all, by Professor Stephen Hawkins, renowned world-wide for his achievements in scientific discoveries, despite his extremely serious disability. Having a strong belief that something GOOD is going to happen in your life appears to actually influence that belief to happen.

Not convinced? A word in the English dictionary that is not **so** widely known is 'placebo'. The interpretation in my dictionary is 'a sugar pill given to unsuspecting patients as an <u>active</u> drug'. There are many cases, where taking this pill actually <u>cures,</u> without the patient knowing it is a 'dummy' pill. (Apologies to the medical professions!) Coincidence, perhaps? But if this is so, why is it prescribed in the first place? The reason is that if the patient <u>actually believes</u> it will cure the illness, **it actually does**!

History is littered with examples which back up the view that the brain itself can do much more than we realise. Without wishing to offend against any religions, the Christian Bible (and other religious sources) quotes such saying as, "God created man in his own image," and "Know ye not that you are gods?" Still not convinced? Then consider the following quotations:

- "Imagination is everything. It is the preview of life's coming attractions." (Albert Einstein)
- "You create your own universe as you go along." (Winston Churchill)
- "All that we are, is the result of what we have thought." (Buddha)
- "Take your first step in faith. You do not have to see the whole journey. Just take the first step." (Martin Luther King Jr)
- "Whatever the (human) mind can create, it will achieve." (W Clement Stone)

The stronger we accept these beliefs and put them into practice, the greater positive effects on your life will occur. So, firstly, stop imagining or visualising future '**unhappiness, debts, and problems**'. Start visualising '**the characteristics of a much happier and successful future for yourself**'. Your brain is basically no different to those people who have made major discoveries in science, created beautiful pieces of art, became famous public figures or made fortunes in business.

So, what does this all mean? It means that whatever problematical situation you find yourself in at the present time, you already have all the equipment required to change the current position, around to whatever better state you want. In taking the route/steps suggested shortly, <u>keep believing, you **will** achieve the success you want and desire.</u>

<u>You now have the opportunity to do this!</u>

<u>Reprogramming your (computer) brain.</u> We considered, previously, how past events can act as restrictions to your self-image and self-confidence, positively or negatively. We noted that many of these events may be lost in our subconscious mind yet still influence our own image. We particularly mentioned the additional negative influences which can affect your confidence levels arising from the actual experience of unemployment

What we can now do is to start to overwrite/re-programme some of the old limitations about yourself possible, by adopting new beliefs into your own brains 'data banks'. In this way, we can begin to correct or remove previously held negative views upon our personalities and work/occupational skills. We start by answering the question: 'what are my weaknesses and inabilities, in a working environment?' For example:

- Do I find it difficult working in a team?
- Do I allow myself to be side-tracked away from central themes?
- Do I have a poor memory?
- Am I untidy in my appearance or in my work?
- Do I listen to other people's opinions or ignore them?

What you are seeking to do is to list, say 5 areas, for improvement, of your own choice. Be honest with yourself, even blunt, and do not try to avoid unpleasant conclusions about yourself. You will be doing this exercise mainly on your own, so you can afford to be realistic. If, however, you have some difficulty in locating 5 areas for self-improvement from your own recollections, then ask a trusted friend/colleague for their views in confidence, and assure them, of course, that there will be no reprisals if they are blunt! If you <u>still</u> have difficulty in doing this exercise, you might refer to section three of this book, where I offer 20 suggestions for 'making a success of the new occupation' which you <u>WILL</u> be obtaining. Ask yourself if, in your old job, there might have been one or two areas within this list, where you may not have performed satisfactorily. Keep a note of them and write a list of statements, but in a way <u>which **reverses** each negative statement</u>. For example, using the statements <u>above</u>, these will now appear as follows:

- **I am** able to work equally well on my own OR as an active and useful member of a team.

- **I have an excellent memory**, and can recall important memories quickly and accurately.
- **I AM tidy in my appearance** both in my standard of dress and in my work.
- **I listen to every person's opinions and statements**, and seriously consider them, even if they are contrary to my own.
- **I care about people** and whenever I can effectively help somebody, I do so, without any expectation of reward.

THEN, whenever you are in your own company, repeat these statements to yourself and BELIEVE what you are saying. Even when you are in the company of others, without being 'distant', and in your own 'world', remember the statements in your own mind. By doing this over a period of time, you are making the changes needed to improve YOU, as a person.

It is, at this time, that you might also establish the nature of your future success in your work, occupation, and personal life. Again, by way of example, think about making—to yourself—the following statements:

- Within the next three years, **I will earn** real promotion, and higher earnings through my work quality, occupational competence, support for others, and my popularity with all my working colleagues.
- **I will establish a high reputation** for my contribution to the success and standing of my employing organisation
- **I will become extensively experienced** and officially qualified and recognised in my chosen occupation.
- **I will earn a high reputation** for my honesty, reliability and integrity.

You should now have a complete list of important areas personal to yourself for 'mind reprogramming'. You need to review and remind yourself, at regular intervals, of these areas. The whole purpose of this exercise is to bring out most, if not all, of your previously held limitations, inadequacies, weaknesses and fears, to **'dump' them**, and replace them with a new set of more positive aspects of **YOU,** as a person. <u>Keep this activity to yourself.</u> Share it with no one. It is work you are doing for yourself and if you carry out this activity, you are more likely to deal with your own past (unjustified?) self-limitations. You will not have other people's doubts or pessimism's reducing your growing self-confidence.

Feeding Your Brain and Maintaining Your Body

"Pick yourself up, dust yourself down, love, and get on with your life" was a piece of advice that my very dear mother once gave me in the early stages of my employment. Later experiences taught me how to apply that rule. Put simply, in addition to 'reprogramming your minds software', you also need (really as a permanent habit) to take practical steps to <u>keep yourself in shape physically and mentally.</u> How do we do this? It is <u>not</u> 'rocket science'.

In respect of <u>feeding your mind</u>, consider the following options, some of which you might already do:

- Library visits. Reference sections, newspapers, periodicals, career publications, specialist/trade magazines and areas of interest books (science fiction, crime stories, romance, geography, history etc.), relevant TV documentary programmes.
- 'Web research' in areas of interest, (after careful selection of the 'key words').
- Evening classes, study periods.
- Voluntary work in carefully selected areas
- Visiting sites of interest. (E.g. castles, museums, 'open days', interest tours etc.)

Studying and updating your work/occupation skills is additional activity which should be done during your (increased) 'free time'. Read up on the latest techniques in your trade or profession, learn a foreign language, improve your IT knowledge are all useful activities at this time.

In respect of your health and fitness, (again, not 'rocket science'). Consider the following new or existing activities/options, some of which you might already do:

- Swimming. In my own view, the best exercise of all. If you cannot swim, join a swimming class, then, go swimming regularly.
- Walks and hiking.
- Diet improvements.
- Health centre activities.
- Football, cricket, tennis. Etc. etc.

The list is endless but pick the ones you enjoy most. A secondary benefit when carrying out physical activities is that you also develop your circle of friends and as mentioned, it is vital for you to maintain regular contact with other people. There is the third benefit. As has already been mentioned, physical exercise is a stress/worry 'buster'. Recall that when you become physically tied, you automatically, relax your mind as well as your body. There are two other matters which you need to bear in mind at this stage. Personal hygiene, and dietary regulation. Both are self-explanatory and further advice is readily available from a variety of different sources. Sufficient to say that through exercise, personal hygiene, and dietary regulation, you are doing what you can to 'keep in shape'.

Reviewing Your Financial Situation

We need now, at this stage, to discuss a financial 'survival plan' whilst you are unemployed. This is another matter which you cannot put to one side! Your work in rebuilding your employment and your future life must not be distracted by threatening correspondence from banks, landlords, building society's and others. The changes in your financial circumstances have to be examined (month by month) in detail. Let's see how you might do this.

In **monthly** terms, firstly identify and note what reliable income you can count on, and what 'occasional' income is possible. Secondly, identify and note, in order of priority, all the items of monthly essential expenditure you currently have. The two columns are then listed, side by side. The intention here is to relate reliable income to the most important items of expenditure. This simple review would then look something like this (ignore the figures!):

INCOME (reliable/guaranteed)		**EXPENDITURE** (essential)	
Unemployment benefits	£600	Mortgage/rent	£300
Partners (P/T) earnings	£250	Rates, water, gas/elect	£100
		Food/shopping	£200
		Insurance/misc.	£100
Totals (per month)	**£850**		**£700**

Now, we need to add any other items of expenditure and how they might be 'financed'.

Transfer from savings (possibly from a lump sum Redundancy payment from a previous employment)	£150	HP Payments	£150
		Car/petrol	£100
		Phone/TV	£100
Totals	**£1,000**		**£1,050**

In business accounting terms, this kind of review is sometimes called 'sources and applications of funds'. We now see that we have a shortfall of £50 each month and this does not accommodate additional expenditure beyond that listed e.g. Christmas, holidays, presents, house repairs etc. So, the next question is what additional measures can be made to accommodate the shortfall? Here are a few options:

- **On the income side** So far as calculating unemployment benefits (now called 'job seekers allowance') there is a useful 'GOV.UK' website which you can use to establish your eligibility for any additional allowances and the benefits payable in your case, together with an online claim form. Go to 'jobseekers allowance (JSA) – GOV.UK' or visit your nearest job centre.
- **On the expenditure side,** could you re-negotiate the mortgage contract to a longer term for less monthly repayments; can you economise on gas, electricity or shopping; can you cancel payments on the phone/television without a 'penalty' charge; does the local council allow any relief/support for unemployed people?
- So far as Redundancy Payments are concerned, the Citizens Advice Bureau provides very good and up to date information and advice in relation to obtaining redundancy pay and you would be well advised to make early contact with the Local office. Briefly, the important points about redundancy pay are as follows:
1. You can receive two forms of redundancy pay, 'statutory' and 'contractual'. It is normally paid by your former employer. 'Statutory' redundancy pay is specified by law. 'Contractual' redundancy pay is extra money your contract of employment says you are entitled to, on top of 'Statutory' redundancy pay.
2. To be entitled to receive 'Statutory' redundancy pay, you must have worked for your employer for a

minimum of two years; there was a genuine need to make redundancies; and you have been classed as an 'employee'. Certain classes of people in receipt of payments for work cannot be paid 'statutory' redundancy pay.

3. Statutory redundancy pay is based upon the number of full years' employment and three 'age' ranges. It is not subject to tax.

4. 'Contractual' redundancy payments (paid by the employer) are additional payments to 'Statutory' payments and are in accordance with your contract of employment. These payments are taxable.

If you have contributed to a 'private' pension scheme during a period of work with a past employer, you may be able to claim back your contributions to provide additional 'one off' financial help at this time. You will, of course, lose the retirement benefits, so you will need to consider this option carefully. Otherwise, you can transfer these contributions to a future 'private' pension scheme which a future employer provides. Your first step on this option is to make contact with your past employer to obtain more information, assuming of course, that the employer is still in business.

Finally, in the question of the income side, could your bank allow, as a temporary measure, an overdraft; can any transfers from your savings account be increased; do you have any unwanted items of value which you could sell?

One word of caution at this stage; try not, at all costs, to borrow money from loan companies unless you have **absolutely** no other option. They all charge an **obscene** level of interest despite their glossy advertisements, and this is not just your own liability, it can also be someone else's liability, who have to act as 'underwriters' of the debt. The last thing loan companies will explain is the **total** full cost of the interest over the term of the contract and what you will actually pay back to them. I talk from personal experience, not for myself, but as an 'underwriter' for a close relative. Nearly 4 years ago, he borrowed £5,000 and agreed monthly payments of £200. Sure enough, the money was instantly available. What the company failed to make clear was that the interest rate of **49.9%** is **compounded** yearly. <u>Actual</u> result? He now owes approx. £2,300 after 48 payments of £200. He still has another 18 months to pay. I leave you to do the maths! What do <u>you</u> think his final costs will be? I now hear of other examples of even higher interest rates!

Having carried out your monthly income and expenditure review, you now need to advise, as many organisations as required in your own case, that you have been made redundant and as a consequence, your income is very much reduced. Your main street bank <u>must</u> be advised. They, at least, will give somewhat more realistic and sensible advice than the loan companies and will be completely open upon what you need to be aware of. All banks offer some form of 'financial health appraisal' which can be very helpful. It is in their long-term business interests to <u>keep</u> you as a customer, so take their advice and keep to whatever conditions they lay down to assist you through this time. After that, the local council, energy companies, phone/TV, and HP companies (bearing in mind the above paragraph) will also need to be advised. Citizens Advice Offices also give sound and supporting advice. It is free, use them if you identify a problem, for which you cannot see a remedy.

Finally, once you have carried out your review, made any changes you can, and advised all who need to know of your changed circumstances, do please keep a more regular review of your accounts. This was not so important whilst you were employed. **It is now!**

So, now we have dealt with most of the immediate effects of actually becoming unemployed, we can now move on to the **'opportunity'** element of your journey, from a 'disaster' to a new more successful life!

Section Two

Redeployment Work
and Action

There are many different ways by which you can create your own work/action plan, and it is for you to decide which you prefer for yourself. I will, therefore, suggest one complete plan which you can consider and this is set out below. Do adapt it to your own circumstances if you need to.

Your first task in this work is to determine precisely what your redeployment target is. If you are not sure <u>where</u> you want to go, how can you hope to get anywhere? You need to make a 'corporate management decision' about <u>your</u> future. That decision is one of the most important decisions of your whole life. There is an old rule in management philosophies. It is approximately this; **'the quality and effectiveness of management decisions is a direct consequence of the accuracy, relevance and completeness of management INFORMATION, which has been carefully obtained, evaluated and judged and is accurate, relevant, timely and comprehensive'**. A somewhat long and complex rule, but in a nutshell, you must carry out a systematic review of many aspects of your past and present occupations and activities and then form a solid conclusion for the future. Sounds difficult? Not really. Let's go through a number of specific steps through this vitally important part of your journey.

First Considerations/Questions/Options

<u>**The first and MOST IMPORTANT questions which you must ask yourself at this time are:**</u> are you looking for a '<u>**better job**</u>' in your **current** occupation, or a **job** in a

different occupation altogether (accepting that you may need to start at perhaps a 'lower' level)? As a **third** option, do you think that your skills, talents, personality and expertise are good enough to justify looking into the option of **working for yourself**.

If the **first** option is your aim, then, by inference, you are confirming that your current work is of most interest to you; that you gain much satisfaction in the work; that you can demonstrate real ability and skill, and can show some verifiable achievements. You are, thus, of the strong belief that no other occupation would be of interest to you. In this case, your 'CV' (Curriculum Vitae, which we will consider shortly), will only comprise of direct past experience, training and past achievements. You need think little more about this first question, at this time.

If, however, your most recent job includes many tasks and activities that you did **not** like doing, or your past occupation might be regarded as a 'dying trade/activity' (outdated, automation etc.), you may have to consider **changing to a different occupation** altogether. Even if you are a fully trained qualified and certified 'Saggar makers bottom knocker' you are going to have to accept this very worthy occupation is now long since gone! Big decision, but one that only you can take. You need to review what working tasks would give you more enjoyment and satisfaction, and are suitable for you—as a person. Try not to take into account unpleasant experiences in your past job unless they specifically relate to the work itself. This is quite a difficult (but important) review for anyone to undertake. So, let me offer three ways you might do this.

First way. Write down those activities which you enjoyed doing, particularly those where other people noted, positively, your work. Add to this list if you can, the subjects you enjoyed most at school, and the kind of matters you take particular interest in, either through reading, hobbies, on the web, the TV, or social activities. Note down also the kind of activities you disliked most, but bear in mind the preceding comments about the power of the human mind. A fairly comprehensive list of different occupations is given in the Appendix 2. Have a browse through these lists, to try to spot one or two different occupations which relate to your past ('strongest') interests. This way is the quickest, simplest review to do.

In Larry Smiths excellent book *No Fear, No Excuses,* He describes discussions with students upon identifying their 'passions' (work wise) and deals with the question: "How do I pursue my passion, if I do not know what it is?"

Larry asked just four critically important questions to a group of students.

How do you spend your free time?
What kind of books do you like?
What kind of conversations do you enjoy having with others?
What kind of projects do you embark on—by choice?

Larry then quotes three example answers which led to a greater understanding of students 'passions' (and occupations). However, one of these cases was a somewhat lazy student who worked only enough to achieve basic academic success, which he did. That student became a very successful working procedures analyst by achieving known objectives at considerable reduced operating costs! Larry's example clearly showed how logic and evidence can find the work that people LOVE or have a talent for doing in a somewhat surprising and unexpected way.

In **appendix two**, I provide a list, (sorry, rather long and detailed) of many different occupations. Having answered the above four questions, you might quickly scan through a few choices if your answers can be interpreted to produce key descriptive words which are relevant to one or two occupations.

Second way. A more 'scientific' method of doing this exercise, would be to seek out one of the many 'Occupational Interest Psychometric Tests' which can be taken to, more accurately, identify your true working interests. Doing a job which you love and enjoy, almost always means you will do it well, be recognised and appreciated, and so facilitate success and achievement in the future. Ask at your local employment centre for advice and information on these tests. (If they do not offer these tests themselves, they may be able to recommend others who do).

The questions themselves in this test have no 'right' or 'wrong' answers. They often comprise basically of a large number of detailed work tasks from a wide selection of different occupations set out in a <u>very</u> random order. You are asked to carefully rank each one into one of (say) five choices, ranging from 'like, very much' to 'would hate it!' (my words, NOT the test words!).

Some questions can only be answered by using your own intuition rather than from your own direct experience. This is OK. In my view, 'intuition' can be a valuable asset, and should not, therefore, be ignored. Once you have completed the questionnaire, a matrix of your responses is used (manually or 'IT') to identify the <u>specific</u> types of occupations which match your own personal <u>interests.</u> (**Note.** These tests <u>must</u> be given and assessed by a person trained and certified to do so, by an official body. Do check this out.) Consider the conclusions carefully and retain the final report in your file. If you want to explore this aspect even more, you might also investigate whether you could also take an '<u>Occupational</u> **Personality** <u>Psychometric Test</u>', which investigates the relationship between your particular personality and various different occupations. For instance, would someone who is somewhat introverted in his personality/nature make a good salesman? I think not! So, search on the web for 'Occupational <u>Personality</u> Questionnaires', some of which may be freely available.

Yet another test which can be taken, particularly in 'hands on' occupations, is sometimes called an **'ability'** test. This is not any kind of intelligence test. Have you got the dexterity/skill needed to handle small components well and correctly? Could you read and understand a written passage and then answer questions correctly? Can you recognise an inconsistency in a drawing or a picture? I mention these other tests at this time, because they are <u>sometimes</u> actually used during interviews for specialised occupations.

When taking these kinds of tests, some people try to 'fiddle' their answers by answering in a way which <u>they</u> think is the 'best' answer. If you do, then the test will simply identify you as a <u>different </u>person than that, which you really are. Will this <u>really</u> benefit either yourself or your new employer? The best advice is simply DON'T! Use the tests to <u>assist</u> you to obtain that better (and happier) job. Use them honestly and you will receive better guidance <u>for yourself.</u>

Third way on the question of reviewing your own suitability to alternative occupations, is to bear in mind, that it does <u>not</u> follow that if you have been a diesel engineer during the last twelve years, you could never eventually change to, say, a financial management role in an engineering company. Considering any alternative occupations is not a wasteful exercise. As has already been mentioned, the nature and characteristics of the employment market is increasingly changing through 'IT', production technology, systems improvement and market forces. How do you see the future of your recent past occupation developing (or not!) in the future? You have, of course, more chance to maintain and improve your career (measured by status, salary, etc.) by staying in your current occupation than by changing to a totally different job, (where, as mentioned, you might have to start lower down 'the ladder'). However, within your past working life, you always will have what is often described as **'transferable skills'** and the engineer's example above attempts to illustrate this point. Our engineers' technical experience/knowledge can help to re-budget costs by moving funds from a somewhat wasteful technical task to a more productive technical activity. Another example of this might be a one parent mother who has, for some years, successfully brought up two children on her own, with little help from other people. She has <u>managed</u> a home, has <u>budgeted</u> income and expenditure, <u>repaired</u> a damaged chair, she <u>cares</u> for others and so on. Do **you** have certain experiences/skills/talents which would be useful in a more 'interesting' but different occupation than your past job?

Reviewing and Determining Occupational Interests, Etc.

One further point you need to consider is whether a specific <u>academic</u> level is involved (mainly by qualifications) and is needed for your chosen occupation, or whether professional/tradesman training is a requirement. Again, advice from others who are actually working in this job will be needed.

I, personally, am a lover of good music, classical and modern. One particular favourite of mine is *Seek the hero inside of yourself, search for the secrets you hide* from the Group 'M People'. Listen to this through the web on your laptop, both the music but also the lyrics. By going through all the above activities, you are implementing the inspirational message contained in this beautiful piece of music.

Finally, (on this rather long exercise of selecting the **occupation** best suited for yourself), you may also wish to consider whether your occupation (current or new) has a high risk of being lost through automation, development of new systems or simply becoming outdated. This check can be simple, by using a 'web search'. Key words for your search engine might be 'occupations most at risk of automation/becoming outdated'.

The third option, **working for yourself (in your own business)** is such a large change, that it is the subject of an entire book in itself. However, you can begin to ask yourself questions like; are your occupational skills comprehensive and extensive enough; can you manage an organisation and other employees; are you financially competent to control a commercial (profit oriented) business; do you have the financial resources needed to set it up; what is the 'competition' like? These are just a few issues you need to address.

You <u>may</u> be naturally talented in this area without realising it and able to adapt from being an 'employee' to an 'employer'. If you were an employee in a small/medium company, you may have noticed how something could be done better or cheaper. Recall the example mentioned earlier, given to us by Ingvuar Kamprad, the creator of IKEA. I am not sure how true this story is, but I read somewhere that one of his inspirations came when he noticed that one of his sales staff removed the legs of a dining table, in order to get it into the customers car boot! Could this be true? That a small incident like this actually resulted in a world-wide business? It could just be so! However, there are many very worthwhile books and publications available in libraries and in bookshops on this subject. You can also obtain advice from specialist organisations and 'Main Street' banks, so I strongly recommend you carry out extensive research, using these sources of help, if you decide to take up this option. However, some parts of this book may still be of help in 'picking yourself up, dusting yourself down, and moving on' AND there is nothing to stop you exploring the options of remaining an employee, at the same time as considering setting up your own business.

OK. Let's now move on to the next tasks in your **Action Plan,** for a new, and better occupation, (as an **employee).** This is after you have carefully addressed the question upon the occupation you need to aim for.

Create or Update Your Curriculum Vitae

- (A basic form of 'CV' is given later in this section). As you will know, your CV shows your complete occupational history, sometimes in great detail. In the past, one would send the complete CV to any and all employers as the application for an appointment. Nowadays, it is becoming different. Firstly, I always recommend that to have 'the full' CV on file is still useful, provided it is comprehensive and accurate, up to date and includes every single occupation/activity/training course carried out so far. But it serves only as a file record for your use only. Whenever an employer asks you to submit a CV, the increasingly popular type is a two-page A4, with a CV '**summary**' of past career information, which is **directly related to the job/work** described in the job description only. There is no benefit to be obtained by listing past activities which have no direct (or indirect) relevance to the job you are applying for. The information should be recorded on **both** pages of the A/4 CV summary, with perhaps a 'shop window' front page. An example CV is given shortly under 'marketing yourself'. If you feel that you need more detailed advice upon 'CV's', again, the web provides many suggestions (too many, for my liking). But have a browse through. The most helpful site, (in my view), was one which gave 'Do's and Don'ts' advice. A **covering letter** with your CV, 'nicely' worded, mentioning briefly any particular past achievements, or verifiable talents in anything to do with the particular job you are interested in, is normally used today. If you have taken any psychometric tests mentioned earlier and the conclusions add weight to your submission, quote the results in your CV submission. Again, a suggested format for a covering letter is given later in this section. Other employers are also moving increasingly to 'online' applications, which ask direct questions for you to answer and submit via e-mail. Your own 'full' CV record can still be useful in this case, as well, for selecting out irrelevant information.

Referees

- **<u>Identify 2/3 people who would be willing (and competent) to give supporting references.</u>** First importance, is your past working life, hopefully mentioning your (relevant) strengths, talents, achievements and personality. Of secondary importance is your <u>personal</u> attributes, like honesty, friendliness, interests and hobbies, in other words, you, as a person. Do check beforehand their willingness to do this if called upon to do so. You <u>might</u> consider asking potential employers to <u>only</u> approach your referees if they are proposing to actually offer you the appointment. This saves your referees work.

You should now have enough information to **start your search for your new occupation.** This will depend, to some extent, on where you live (city or rural), but the following list summarises your search areas:

- Local job centres who can give advice and information upon actual vacancies and a schedule of local employment agencies, in addition to their other services, by arrangement.
- Local employment agencies. Information received from the job centre, about the local job agencies, very often tells you about the types of jobs/occupation the particular agency specialises in. Compare this list with the conclusions you reached about job interests for yourself and you will have the contact details of local employer agencies to contact to enlist their support in your job search. You may need to register with an agency, but this is normally at no cost to yourself.
- Advertisements in the press. Both the local and national press carry advertisements for vacancies. Clearly, the national press is likely to attract much more competition than the local press. Recruiting is advertised on particular days of the week.
- Local Employers. Direct Contacting. If you have been able to identify your best occupational interests/abilities, you can relate this information on a 'web search' using key words to your search engine, e.g. 'TV engineers, Northampton'. You need to identify those employer's that do employ people with your background, interests and talents. Thereby, you are in a position to send 'speculative' enquiry letters, with your CV summary, asking if they have any current vacancies in your own preferred occupation. Do bear in mind that it is often claimed that **at least**

two thirds of all vacancies are not advertised because many employers see the benefits of recruiting within their organisation. Should you, therefore, ignore this position? I think NOT. If you do, you will be potentially turning a blind eye to many opportunities.

- Employment Development Areas. In all towns and cities, new areas are being set aside and developed for all types of employers. You might seek out the ones which are fully built and are in the process of occupation. Establish the organisations name, and check from the web if their activities are relevant to your own occupational interests. If they are, note these down for a possible speculative enquiry. (See the later section on this subject.)

- Family and friends. In Section One, I mentioned the value and importance of maintaining contacts socially, whether they be family, friends, of acquaintances from interests, activities or sports clubs. The first reason for this is to maintain your 'social circle', which is important whenever someone is dealing with one of life's problems. In the matter of dealing with unemployment, I have heard of a few cases where an unemployed person has taken many of the steps listed above, but these have not helped. But 'out of the blue', a new job was obtained through news from a friend. So one further way of job searching is to let everyone know you are seeking a new job, but also tell them the kind of occupation you want. Nothing lost by doing this.

By doing all the above actions, you are widening your options, gaining important information and taking you first steps to improve your life.

As with any new 'campaign' there are essential truths which have to be accepted at the outset. Let us come to terms with the most important aspect straight away. Unless you are very lucky to be in the right place and right time, acquiring a new occupation is going to require commitment, effort and perseverance. You have to accept that you are going to have to put in sustained effort. It is a 'priority one' task. Those who start their redeployment work immediately upon having confirmation of employment termination (or even before) are more likely to obtain a new job, than those who put off this task until 'later'. Having carried out the steps described in the previous pages, and have identified the kind of employment you want to obtain (and the kind of organisation too), you now need to move on to the next stage, to start 'selling yourself'.

But to summarise, **so far**:

- You have carefully reviewed your own personal occupational interests, attributes and abilities, and have concluded what specific jobs you feel are now 'right' for you.
- You have identified sources of information for occupational opportunities.
- You have prepared a 'full' CV, 'summary' CV, qualifications, past achievements, and obtained agreements from 2–3 people who will act as supporting references.

You next tasks will be:

- Seeking actual vacancy opportunities and submitting applications.
- Sending 'speculative' enquiries to appropriate local employers who specialise in your particular area of occupational interests.
- Practice and prepare yourself for interviews.
- Receive and perhaps, negotiate job offers.
- Accept the new appointment.
- And finally, to **SUCCEED** in your new occupation

Big List??? NO! Piece of cake, stroll in the park!

You might not obtain success straight away, but keep your efforts going and you will progressively gain more experience, self-confidence, and knowledge and thereby become more proficient in these tasks.

'MARKETING YOURSELF'

Once you have carried out the important tasks described in the preceding section, you can now move onto the next stage, this being making contact with employers and 'selling yourself'. But as a starter, **you need to create a well-maintained record system** which stores records of <u>all</u>-important actions which you will now be taking in an organised and clear way. I remember a piece of advice which a rather attractive female lecturer gave to me many years ago. She told me to remember the word 'KISS'. **Alas,** no amorous intent was involved! The interpretation for my benefit was 'keep it simple, stupid!' (I am still trying to do this!). However, <u>with no offence intended</u>, I pass on this piece of good advice.

In deciding the format of your record system, determine for yourself from your experience in 'IT' systems and software how you would prefer to set up your own system. Are you familiar with 'word' systems, e-mailing documents, spread sheets and other basic 'IT' procedures? I will not delve into what system you choose, but I will suggest the following list of **records sections**. Select the ones you think are appropriate to you:

- **Curriculum Vitae (main version)** containing **all information** concerning past jobs, work carried out, training and qualifications, achievements, hobbies, references, and <u>full</u> contact information (for yourself). This needs regular review and updating.
- **Copies of 'summary CV's' submitted to employers**, with covering letters, together with details of the jobs applied for (job descriptions) with a note of results. (Every summary sent to an employer <u>must</u> only relate to the stated requirements of the position and is consequently an 'extract' from your CV main version). Each summary submitted will be different as it will be 'tailored' to relate to each job description.

- **Qualification certificates, past supporting reference letters**, and evidence of past achievements/acknowledgements of your work.
- The **results from any psychometric tests** mentioned earlier, if you have these.
- **List of <u>local employers</u>** recruiting in your chosen 'occupational area' (For speculative enquiries).
- Records of contact with **<u>employment agencies</u>, <u>job centres</u>**.
- **Notes of your own experiences** which help to make your efforts/work, **<u>better.</u>**

Hopefully, by regularly checking all the sources of vacancy information given previously (job centres, employment agencies etc.), you will now be receiving a reasonable supply of occupational opportunities. Some information sources may prove to be of little use. You need to make your own judgement upon whether to use them or delete them. You will be considering all vacancy information carefully in respect of their relationship to your chosen jobs to identify which to go for. If you find that you are not locating many jobs which suit you, <u>after a reasonable period of time</u>, you may need to go back to your past work in identifying the occupations which meet your interests, abilities and personality, and try to amend your aims, taking into account the information and experience you are now receiving. However, this is hopefully, <u>not</u> the case and some of the vacancies will match your needs.

When you find a particular vacancy that interests you, you will normally request and receive further job information from the selected employers which describes the work in greater detail <u>and</u> the way applications should be made. Read the employers job information <u>very</u> carefully. Can you satisfy at least 60% of the criteria for selection? If so, start preparing your bid.

You need to follow the employer's instructions for submission of applications fully, and to carefully create a summary 'CV' which matches the jobs requirements <u>directly</u>

in respect of the positions work/training requirements. If submitting your application/CV by letter (hard copy), **a covering letter <u>might</u>** be along the following lines. If applying by e-mail, the suggested letter's wording may still be appropriate. (Of course, you will need to amend the names and addresses details!). A suggested CV style follows for the covering letter:

Example Covering Letter / CVs

From: Mickey Pluto   27, The Scuffy Hovels,

           Home phone 0123456   Old Sewage Works Lane

           Mobile phone 6543210   Noway Town,

           E-mail, etc., 98765   Hopelessshire

To: The Director of Human Resources
        XYZ Enterprises Incorporated Ltd
        Loverly Gardens Lane,
        VeryposhTown
        Heavenshire

<u>(Now for the serious part!)</u>

Dear Madam,

Appointment of (Say) Landscape Advisor

Thank you for sending the details of the above vacancy. After careful consideration, I would very much like to be considered for this appointment.

During my work for my two most recent employers, I have completely redesigned the Local Councils Park Lane Recreation and Sports Ground which has now earned the Department of Environments National Award for a Public Amenity of Outstanding Quality: identified and rectified a rare tree disease in Hopingwood Forest; and reduced maintenance costs of Central Park by 40% with no loss of amenities. I am a Fellow of the Horticultural Society and have published two national papers in the Institute's Annual Report (2012. 2016).

A CV summary of the most relevant aspects of my career, to the requirements of your vacancy, is attached together with the contact details of two persons who are willing to provide supporting references.

I do hope my application is of interest. I should mention I will be abroad on holiday between 14th and 25th March 2018.

Yours sincerely,

As an alternative to the 'text style' of the second paragraph, you could use 'bullet points' instead. As mentioned earlier, a search on the web (under 'CV keywords') will provide the most effective words for you to use in your application e.g. 'adaptable', 'achieved', 'implemented', 'generated'. Do use these when you can, <u>but be sure you are able to justify them at an interview in your own case.</u> If you have been responsible for – say – 'transport administration', <u>you might, for instance, be able to say</u>:

- Formulated and managed a successful strategy for dealing with persistent delivery problems.

OR

- Designed a successful database for monitoring all aspects of delivery performance against specified targets.

I see from one test run on the web that employers are increasingly using IT software for evaluating job applications. Not too sure about the wisdom of this. The software looks for particular words only, which may reject many well-worthy candidates (for the work itself) who are not too familiar with submitting 'good' job applications.

(Front cover title page printed one side only)

Curriculum Vitae

Appointment of new housing plumber
W H Bentley Building Co Ltd

Thomas Frederick Harrison
Nottingham

Executive Summary

I am a fuller qualified (e.g. Plumber) with 15 years extensive experience in fitting comprehensive systems to new house builds including all hot/cold water and central heating provisions and all plumbing requirements to bathrooms and kitchens.

CV Contents

Identity contact details, education and training

Relevant past employment details

Interests, hobbies and references

(Second page,)

Identity/Contact Details

Full name:
Address:
Phone contacts;   (home/mobile)
E-mail address:
Nationality:
Date of birth:

Education and Training

Dates   School/College   Training/qualification

Certificates/Qualifications

(All will be available for inspection at interview if required)

(Third page printed either on the back of page two or as a separate page. A fourth page can be added if needed)

Current, Past Employment

Dates   Employer   Job title

For each employment give a one paragraph description of the main job functions and responsibilities

Interests and Hobbies

This section would include interests/hobbies/part-time activities which show either some relevance to the particular occupation involved, or activities which show other positive aspects of you as a person. Such things as amateur football club secretary, voluntary work for others, or photography.

References

(Full names and addresses of two competent Referees who have agreed to support your application)

Sending Speculative Enquiries

Despite all your efforts in responding to openly advertised vacancies, from employment agencies, newspaper advertisements etc. you can also access the market for those <u>unadvertised jobs</u>, and to send speculative enquiries to organisations who clearly recruit in your chosen, preferred occupational area. How do you do this? It is, actually, fairly simple by (again) carrying out a 'web search'. <u>As a practice run</u>, pick out say, three randomly selected occupations. Open up the 'web' and type the '<u>key</u>' words of (e.g.) – '<u>Beauty Therapist</u>' (or 'Carpet Fitter', or 'Plant Mechanic'), then '<u>vacancies</u>', then '<u>Southampton</u>' (or 'Birmingham', or 'Liverpool'). More often than not, you will have the names of employers recruiting in that field, and details of actual vacancies, mainly through employment agencies. Where the employers <u>contact</u> details are not given, the web will give you their address, phone numbers and e-mail address by a separate search. Do this then <u>for your own occupation</u> choice and location, and you will have the contact details you need to circulate your enquiries to, either by post, or by e-mail to the employers you have identified. If the list is on the small side, you could, depending upon your own circumstances, <u>widen</u> the geographical area and search again.

Once you have identified and chosen one or two employers, how would you 'word' your enquiry? This is very much influenced by the type of occupation you are seeking. But one example might be as follows:

(By e-mail or by letter)

Dear Sir/Madam,

<u>Employment Enquiry</u>
<u>New Housing Plumbers</u>

I am currently looking for a new appointment in the above occupation, and following a search on the web, I see that you may be regularly employing experienced plumbers for new housing projects.

I am a fully qualified plumber, with over 20 years' experience, in fitting comprehensive systems to new house builds, including all hot/cold water and central heating provisions and all plumbing work associated with bathrooms, and kitchens. I can provide references from past employers and copies of my qualification and training certificates. I enjoy good health, and have a full, clean, driving licence. I would be available to start, if required, from 31st March, 2019.

If you have any current vacancies, perhaps you would let me know, please. If not, perhaps you might be willing to retain this enquiry on file for any future vacancies which arise. My contact details are above (or, set out below if sending an e-mail).

I look forward to hearing from you.

Yours Sincerely,
John Smith.

So, you have now reached the point on your travels along our **route** where you are searching for vacancies and potential opportunities, and submitting well-prepared applications, CV's and speculative enquiries. You will be <u>earning</u> the opportunity of interviews (much more on that shortly). You will also be receiving ('nicely worded' rejections). And the danger here is that you might be experiencing another 'dip' in your level of self-confidence. <u>Don't allow this to happen!</u> You have already come a long way along the route and have probably got over some quite difficult times. Use any rejections as **'fuel'** to <u>enforce</u> your determination and belief in yourself.

However, you also may feel that that you have done enough at present, and have submitted a reasonable number of applications and speculative enquiries. You can now relax, sit back, and just keep sending in the applications. My advice is for you to try to find the time to <u>start</u> to prepare for the next part of your journey. That is 'the job interview'. <u>In doing so, you may uncover ideas for more improvement to your approaches to new employers.</u>

Interview Preparation and Performance

Having now submitted a number of well-prepared job applications and speculative enquiries, you are, hopefully, starting to receive invitations to attend interviews. So, interview preparation and performance now become the next essential part of your journey.

I am, therefore, dividing this section into the two main parts. Firstly, the preparations you should take before the actual interview, and then, secondly, anticipating how the actual interview itself will be conducted, with particular reference to how best to present yourself, likely questions which you may be asked, what points **you** want to get over during the interview, plus any questions which **you** would like to ask (if given the opportunity to do so) which clarifies issues which may be of concern to you. However, before this, it is important to understand a few general points about recruiting interviews.

Between the time of submitting your CV/application and the receipt of an invitation to an interview, some employers nowadays carry out a preliminary selection exercise by phone. Each case is different, but the general idea is to clear up, before the final decision on the 'short list', some routine aspects of your past life/work. This is also in order to give more time for more important aspects to be discussed during the actual interview. Have a think about this after posting/emailing your application and keep your mobile phone with you at all times if you have one and you have given this number in your application/CV. You should be able to answer straight-forward questions about your past occupational life, possibly from you main CV file which includes detailed information. More involved questions are not normally asked during this preliminary contact. If they are asked, tell the caller (politely of course) that you will ring them back with your response. This is also a way of giving you the chance to consider your response carefully and also to verify the identity of the caller!

I have heard of a few cases where the candidate's **performance, during the interview itself,** is sometimes given an excessive amount of consideration, than the question of the candidate's actual occupational abilities for the work, their interests and personality. It is absolutely right for you to demonstrate a reasonable performance at the interview, which is why we have considered this need, in detail. The most important thing from the employers' point of view, however, is that the selected candidate is able to do the actual job well and experienced interviewers will make allowances for the odd slip by the Interviewee. Unless this kind of communication ability (e.g. 'negotiating') is important in the work involved in the job, it is a fault of the recruiting interviewer by just considering interview performance. Where an employer makes this mistake, they may well suffer the consequences in the future. Additionally, if this was the case, would you have the same enthusiasm for the job if you knew this interviewing approach had been applied? And don't forget, by carefully carrying out your self-evaluation of your occupational interests, abilities and personality, you will still be more confident about the direction you are taking, on this journey. However, it **is** still important for you to present yourself in the 'best light', and we will consider this, in greater detail, shortly.

No candidate for interview ever 'loses' by being interviewed for a job they do not get. You have carried out a systematic review of your occupational aspirations. You have prepared a detailed and relevant CV. Your application was good enough to be considered worthy of an interview. You will have acquired first-hand experience of the recruiting interview experience. You will know more about yourself, where you were confident during the meeting, and where you struggled in your performance. Knowing any such problems means that you are half way towards solving them

There is no general rule upon the make-up of the employer's interview arrangements, particularly who you will be interviewed by. Clearly, the more senior appointments will involve an interview panel, comprising (say), the company director, chief executive, line manager and personnel manager. A junior appointment, (e.g. office trainee, trainee electrician), may only include the supervisor/manager and a personnel officer. This should not change your preparations or how you present yourself at the interview. Simply judge for yourself who might interview you based upon the level/importance of the actual vacancy.

Finally, on the question of general considerations, it needs to be emphasised that the time between receiving the invitation to attend the interview and the interview itself, must be where you allocate time to plan and practise your interview performance. (Remember the 5/6 'P's' rule! (Practice and preparation prevents (!!!) poor performance.) It means you will need to distance yourself from family and friends and withdraw, without being too 'anti-social'. Explain, openly, what you are doing. They will understand. Whilst doing this exercise, you should also start to collect a few papers/documents for taking to the interview. For instance:-

- Copies of your CV and covering letter, submitted to the employer.
- Employer's invitation to attend the interview.
- Job/vacancy information (most important).
- Copies of any website information you have obtained about the employer (which you will 'casually' set out before you during the interview. This always scores points!). (Note for employers: you have **not** read this!)
- Qualifications/certificates
- Your own notes about the vacancy, with questions you may need to clarify at the interview.

Interview Arrangements / Typical Questions

Preparations before the interview. There are a number of essential actions you need to do before the day of the interview. For the sake of clarity, use the following as a quick check list.

- Within the job information papers, you will, almost always, have a description of various forms of past experience, training and qualifications which the employer will be seeking in order to select the successful candidate. You will have considered this information before submitting your application and have included some reference to it in your CV. Now that you have been selected for the interview, <u>you need to define, in greater detail, exactly how you meet each</u> requirement. Do not wait to be asked this at the interview without prior preparation. I suggest you take with you to the interview a paper on which you have written notes upon your <u>detailed</u> past experience, training, talents, achievements and any psychometric test results which relate to each specified job requirements given in the information paper.

- Check the <u>location of the interview premises.</u> This may mean, if necessary, doing a dummy run a few days beforehand. Check and plan the route and travelling time. Aim to arrive 10 minutes before your allocated interview time, NOT less than 5 minutes, NOT more than 15 minutes. The reason for this rather exact advice is that for many people, 10 minutes before the interview, guarantees you arrive on time, you have time to 'settle' and gather your composure, but not too much time to get stressed. In doing a dummy run, check the immediate neighbourhood for any possible congestion points and parking facilities.

- <u>Dress.</u> The general rule is 'smart/casual', with no 'excessiveness'. Feel free (<u>normally</u>) to have multi-coloured hair, ear studs all over the place, tattoos all over your head, torn and ripped garden jeans and <u>one</u>

eye fully made up (and that's the males!), but NOT for an interview which may benefit the rest of your life!

- Put together <u>your own interview file</u> comprising the job details from the employer, a copy of your CV and covering letter, and any up to date literature you have found about the employer (or the 'trade') from the press or the web (which, recall, you will 'casually display'). I use a simple, flat, two cover clip file, which is easy to carry and normally holds enough papers for meetings of this type. Also, of course, include your prepared notes on how, <u>in detail,</u> you meet the criterion for selection in the job information pack.

- **Finally,** include, in your own interview file, a <u>note of a couple of sensible questions which you would ask</u> if you are given the opportunity to do so, at the conclusion of the interview. This can be important. It shows you to be a candidate who has looked into this vacancy to some depth. <u>Make sure your questions relate directly to some working aspect of the job.</u> (NOT 'is there a licensed bar in the works canteen?'!). Also check that the answers are not <u>already provided</u> in the job papers supplied by the employer. Finally, be ready to <u>give a reason</u> why you asked the question.

OK, so now we have completed all the preceding steps we now move on to the interview itself.

Your Interview Presentation/Performance

There are many books and websites on the market which give a wealth of good advice and guidance on this subject. However, this book would not be complete if only little reference was included in a vitally important aspect of your journey. I have previously advised you to exercise your mind in tackling the wide variety of interview questions given in the book's appendix. If you do have time, after receiving the invitation to attend an interview, to have a go at dealing with some more example questions, do so, <u>but not on the day of the interview itself</u>

Again, with apologies to my readers who already have good experience in attending interviews, another 'check list' of information, concerning the standard procedures which you often follow before, during and after the actual interview.

- **On arrival**, you report to the designated reception point (10 minutes before the interview time) and introduce yourself to the receptionist as a candidate for interview for the appointment of (e.g. 'foreman plumber') vacancy. Smile and speak clearly and confidently. In some cases, your interview may have already commenced!

- Normally, you will be shown to a designated **waiting area**, and perhaps be given up to date information upon the interview arrangements. Take careful note of this. Having arrived a little early, you give yourself time to settle your mind, check your file of papers, and take in the surroundings. Hopefully not too much time for you to get stressed!

- One of the interviewing panel (if it is a selection panel interview) will then **collect you and take you into the interview room.** You will be introduced to the interviewers with their names. Try to remember these if you can, smile at each one with 'hello', then take your seat and open up your own interview file. It is often a nice opening gesture at this point for you to perhaps simply say: 'Thank you for seeing me'.

- **The senior panel member will then take charge of the interview,** and may explain the format of the interview. If it is a panel interview, it is usual for each panel member to ask their own pre-arranged interview questions. Always give your answers direct to the interviewer who asked them, with occasional glances to other panel members. Try to remain relaxed throughout. Remember, <u>you are the possessor of skills and experience which the employer has already officially confirmed may be useful to the employing organisation</u>. It is during the main part of the interview where you will use your prepared responses and other thoughts which come to you during the meeting. You will, of course, be asked questions which you have not anticipated and have not prepared ready-made answers. This is the reason for providing sample interview questions given in Appendix 1. If you have practised answering some of these questions beforehand, you will have gained some experience in giving good 'off the top of your head' responses, during the actual interview. It is possible that you could be asked a question which you simply cannot answer. This might be because you have no past experience in the subject of the question, OR you have no views or opinions about the subject raised. Rather than give a 'guesstimate' response, I think it would be better, after a pause, to admit openly that at present, you have no past experience in the subject of the question. However, given more time to look into the point raised, you feel confident you would be able, both to extend your experience/knowledge and after a short time, "perform satisfactorily". This kind of response would display to the interviewers at least honesty and openness and should not therefore be regarded unkindly.

- **<u>At the end of questions by the panel/interviewers,</u>** you are normally asked if you have any questions for the panel. If this happens rummage through your file of papers (perhaps at this stage casually putting down any printed 'web' information about the organisation!) and take out the note paper containing the couple of questions you have prepared beforehand. <u>Unless they have been answered already</u>

<u>during the interview,</u> ask the questions and briefly note their answers.

- **Finally,** you will be thanked for attending the interview and possibly be advised when and how the final decision will be communicated to candidates. Whatever your experience has been in the interview, <u>thank the interviewers for giving you the opportunity of the interview</u>, smile (again) and wish them (e.g.) 'Good afternoon' and leave the interview room. Pay your respects to the receptionist to whom you may have reported on arrival, smile and leave the building.
- **As soon as possible, after the interview,** note down your impressions, of the interview generally, where you think you 'scored', and where you struggled a little, and why. This information may well develop your interviewing skills for next time, if this particular interview proves to be unsuccessful.

To my mind, there are four principle question area's which will arise in all recruiting interviews. These are as follows:

1. **Summarise why you think you are suitable for this appointment**. Hopefully, you have partially answered this already in you CV, but you will need to elaborate on your past working experience, your training and qualifications. If you have mentioned in your CV past <u>achievements</u>, give more details. If you have taken any psychometric tests (as recommended earlier), quote the test and the results, to provide more reasons why you are suitable. And, of course, you have your prepared interview notes mentioned above.

2. **Explain how your occupational knowledge and experience can be useful to the company.** This is a slightly unfair question unless you have <u>inside</u> information and details of the work. However, since, in your preparations for the interview, you have already worked on the printed job description ('essential' and 'desirable' requirements) you should be reasonably

prepared for this question. Refer again to your interview notes but also ask yourself (before the interview) if, during your research upon the employer, you have identified something of their work and activities which is of particular interest to you. In this case, mention what you have found and why this information is of interest to you. End by making the point that in any 'changed job situation' there are always new things to learn. <u>You have the benefit of a 'fresh' mind to deal with any occasional shortcomings which you are honest enough to accept (nobody is perfect!).</u> This is often a <u>strength</u>, rather than a weakness.

3. **<u>How motivated are you for this position?</u>** This is one of those interview questions where you should <u>pause</u> for a brief moment (directly looking at the questioner, before giving your answer). If you do this for this question (or others), you convey to the panel that you are taking time to <u>think</u> before giving a quick ('rash') response. <u>Then</u> perhaps start with an answer along the following lines: 'I do not apply for jobs unless I am strongly confident that my interests, experience and talents will provide not only <u>personal</u> satisfaction, but equally important, real benefits to a new employer. (Your) work principle is simply to go 'the extra mile' to achieve success for both my employer and myself. In this respect, for instance, I would initially at least, arrive earlier for work and leave later without any expectation of reward. I would then become more quickly familiar with both the demands of the job and the general circumstances of working for my new employer. I strongly want this appointment and will do whatever I can to make it successful and to fully justify <u>your</u> decision to appoint me.' If, for example, additional training becomes necessary, I would be willing to do this in my own time by research on the web, or in specialised publications. You could also add that you have ambitions to reach higher occupational

levels later, and to do this you will need to EARN a high reputation in your work. (Again, if you have <u>positive</u> psychometric test results, use them too).

4. **<u>Can you provide a little more information upon your work with the XYZ company mentioned in your CV and why you left this position?</u>** This is a tricky one which will need a careful response. Try to concentrate upon the actual work angle in a positive way and that you left for purely 'perceived' career progression reasons or, of course, because of redundancy. **<u>Never, ever, criticise a past employer.</u>**

One aspect of being interviewed which many people do not appreciate is that interviewers are **people** with both, strengths and weaknesses, personal interests, opinions and prejudices (like you and I). The result is that sometimes they ask a candidate questions which are surprising, unexpected and difficult to answer immediately. In **Appendix 1,** therefore, is listed a variety of such questions. This can give you some prior practice in dealing with unexpected points raised by interviewers. Have a glance at a few and consider how you would respond if asked the questions you pick.

As mentioned earlier, the web is full of very useful advice upon interview performance. Tips about 'Do's and Don'ts', are of particular help. My own list, based upon past experience from **both sides** of the interview table, is as follows.

- Whatever time is allocated to you, allow extra time both before and after the interview.
- During the interview, listen out for areas of common interest between the interviewers and yourself and then extend your response positively.
- Consider, in your preparation work, where you have realistic thoughts upon <u>development and improvements</u>. Then try to bring them out during the interview as <u>'areas you would like to investigate'</u>, subject, of course, to prior agreement.

- Without being excessively flattering, look for areas where you might compliment the employer for some reason or another, whenever you have a chance.
- Try not to be drawn into arguments. A possible response from you might be to express a provisional view but that you would need further information before coming to a final view. This might arise from additional information which you have found from – say – a prior 'web search'.
- Do not avoid discussing any perceived weaknesses you might have. There should be few anyway because you have been called for an interview. Be positive. Say how you might deal with any possible shortcomings in ways which would benefit both the employer and yourself. Try to anticipate this situation before the interview.
- Do always answer the question to the person who asked it with occasional glances to other interviewers.
- Do not rush into all your responses to questions. Think first before giving an answer. Where you have an 'outstanding' answer already prepared, pause again before giving it. This is certainly a 'merit earning' tactic.

So, I hope the foregoing section is of help in this important hurdle to 'leap over'. Always remember when you are given any interview, **you have the talents and experience the employer may want to buy from you.** Otherwise, you would not be invited to the interview. Let's now move on to the next item; '**Interview Results**'.

Interview Results, Initial Reactions

Obviously, there are two (most likely) consequences following your interview. You were selected for appointment, or you were 'regretted'. There might, in some circumstances, be a <u>third</u> consequence. That is, for some reason or another, the employer has decided NOT to make an appointment. In this case, a responsible employer will give some information to all interviewed candidates upon why this decision has been taken. After all, you and the other interviewees have gone to the trouble of applying for the vacancy and given the time and effort to attend the interview, and this should, at least, be acknowledged with a brief explanation by the employer.

The first consequence, (you were selected for appointment), is obviously excellent news. Apart from anything else, your new self-confidence will be fully justified, your past work in 'picking yourself up, dusting yourself down and getting on with your life' has been rightly rewarded. Your next step, 'succeeding in the new job', is the subject of the final chapter of the book. So, please **do** read on for this final stage of your travels. There are important considerations for you to bear in mind, if you are to finally ensure that this event become a truly successful one.

The second consequence is clearly a disappointing one, but **it is not the end of the world.** You have survived the initial shock of becoming unemployed. You have reminded yourself that, as a person, you have much to offer. You have conducted a comprehensive self-analysis of your past employment, your skills and talents. You have examined your 'shortcomings' and rejected certain doubts about yourself. You have carried out a systematic review of the occupations best suited to your interests, personality and attitudes. You have taken the first steps in securing a new job (job search, CV preparation, making applications/enquiries to employers) and you have now persuaded one employer that you are worthy of serious consideration for an occupation of your choice. And finally, you have prepared yourself for the interview and have given an interview presentation. All this work cannot possibly be regarded as a waste of time. You have regained most of your self-confidence, you have an orderly structured plan of action. You know more about yourself. You have prepared a file of your past work experience, training/qualifications, past achievement (all of which does not have to be done again) and you now have the first-hand experience of interview performance. **You are a better person than you were before.**

So, what are your next steps in dealing with an 'unsuccessful' interview? Consider the following option. If you feel your interview went well, and that you are now even more convinced that this particular occupation is 'right for you', you could send a ('nice') enquiry by letter or e-mail, to the employer asking if they <u>might</u> be willing to provide some guidance upon your strengths and weaknesses. The wording might be along the following lines:

Dear Sir/Madam/Mr Smith,
<u>Appointment of plumber</u>
<u>New housing sites</u>

Thank you for letting me know the results of the interviews for the above appointment. Naturally, I am disappointed with the result, but I accept your judgement and express my thanks again for considering my application. I wonder, however, whether you might be willing/able, to provide me with a little guidance upon any shortfall/inadequacies, in either my CV or my interview performance. This kind of occupation is of particular interest to me and I am anxious to improve and develop my experience, skills and training in order to achieve my objective.

Any tips or advice which you are willing to give (in strict confidence) would be greatly appreciated, either by e-mail or by phone and <u>would be for my own guidance only.</u> They would not be communicated to anyone else. In the meantime, may I again, wish the company every success, in its future business. Thank you again for interviewing me.

Yours sincerely,

Looking back on your performance during the interview, do you feel, yourself, that you either struggled to answer any particular question; felt that a particular interviewer was a little 'hostile' to you (this does happen and it is not your fault); or that it became clear to you that you did not after all, satisfy the selection criterion. Also, did anything come up during the interview which could influence your plans for working in this particular occupational area? Be honest with yourself and be reasonably critical. If this is the case, <u>record your thoughts as notes in your 'Redeployment File'</u>.

During some interviews, new information about the job comes to light, that was not included in the job information papers. Again this is not your fault. It is up to the employer to provide a clear description of the job, its demands, and ideal past experience. Note this down, again in your file perhaps on the actual job information paper.

After doing all the foregoing, you now need to continue your work in seeking new opportunities and submitting applications and enquiries. <u>The sooner you do this, after the interview, the better.</u> (**'Move on my friend, move on!'**). Check your CV to see if it needs amending in any way, based on your recent interview. Continue your search for new opportunities (job centres, newspapers, recruiting agencies, the web, speculative letters etc.) and submit more applications and enquiries. You may feel that your search parameters are too restrictive (e.g. geographical area, occupational descriptions etc.) in which case amend the relevant 'key' words. Remind yourself that on your 'route', you will <u>have</u> to leave the main road, on occasions, to look into a serious possibility for a better life.

It is now necessary to <u>return</u> to the main road/route and continue your journey into your new occupation/job.

Section Three

Future Occupational Successes

Making a Success in the New Occupation

Having now travelled a long and challenging route, you are now standing on the very threshold of a better life. **Commend yourself** for reaching this point. Start to be happy and enjoy your new found self-confidence. However, with all similar achievements, there is often the word '**but**'. All your past efforts could be wasted if you believe you have already reached the winning point (the 'chequered flag') and there is nothing more to do. Before even reporting for work on your first day, there remains (still!) work for you to do. This work comprises of applying new rules and habits in your new working life. There is little point in coming all this way and achieving what you have now achieved, if you 'mess up' in your new job. This you could do, by not doing what you should, and doing what you should not be doing.

On the web, again, there are some very useful publications on the subject of 'succeeding in a new job'. They contain many varied suggestions, all of which do have their merits. Some will have greater or lesser relevance upon various aspects of making a success in your new job and upon different types of occupation. Additionally, there is a marked difference in style between UK authors and those from the USA (I infer NO criticism of either).

Some advice is more appropriate in commercial occupations, but not appropriate in public sector occupations. I have, therefore, attempted to identify 20 fundamental rules for you to consider. They are based upon my own experience and knowledge as a general manager, careers administrative officer, employee redeployment officer through academic studies in the UK and the websites I have researched. I suggest you consider all the rules in the list and, from what you now know of the employer you are about to serve, **prioritise** the rules before you start your new occupation. Then amend the priorities following the first few days/weeks of working. The amendments will be based upon your increased knowledge of the job itself, the targets you need to set for yourself and the people you will be working and associating with.

Bear in mind that this list is NOT prioritised. The points are intentionally listed in a random order. This will enable you to award simple priority classifications immediately (say 'A, B, C, D') in order of your perceived importance, and then amend the classifications on the basis of your growing experience in the job. Be mindful that for each different occupation, different rules apply. Use your own occupational experience to prioritise the most and least important rules.

So, here is the 20-rule listing (again intentionally given random order).

20 Suggested Rules for the New Job

1. **Establish the 'norm' of good working attire,** whether 'occupational' clothing is applied or 'everyday attire'). Without making it obvious, perhaps copy the best dressed, particularly that of more senior employees. Then set this as your regular permanent standard.

2. **Establish the employee's organisational chart.** You need to know the <u>official</u> structure of the organisation. Who is in charge of who, often illustrated by an inverted 'tree' showing basically, the top 'boss', then supervising section heads, and then the workers. This depicts officially, who is responsible to who, from the most 'junior' upward to the most 'senior'. This will be the <u>'official'</u> chart which you need to know at an early stage. Keep this for yourself pinned up on a notice board or as a document in your own IT records. After a few months working, you may begin to recognise an <u>informal</u> organisational arrangement based upon who relates better to others and who doesn't, and important 'cross sectional' lines of communication. Clearly, such kind of knowledge is strictly for your own private use only, possibly for your own protection in how you communicate with others. It will help you not to tread on too many wrong toes and to know who can be trusted and relied on in any confidential matters.

3. **Establish a regular pattern of reviews of your own performance with you supervisor (or mentor).** Your immediate supervisor (and mentor) are clearly in an important position to influence your success in the new job. Obviously, weekly meetings in the first few months is a 'must' where you provide full reports upon your work, (always try to emphasise work <u>accomplished</u> successfully), obtain advice and clarifications and agree next jobs. If you have experienced any difficulties, this is the time to bring them out, but with your own ideas upon how you would deal with them. You must also try to aim at being supportive to your supervisor's <u>own</u> work. Be friendly, absolutely loyal, and try to give help in any way you can (I would strongly advise an 'A' classification for this suggestion).

4. **Be friendly and supportive to all you meet.** Offer the hand of friendship, by introducing who you are, what your position is, shake hands and use first names whenever you can. Keep the conversation constructive and relevant to the work and if appropriate, add a little humour, (carefully worded, of course). Find out what they do in the organisation but do not be too intrusive. Try to find areas of common interest related to working aspects, but perhaps also related to outside interests and pursuits. Your aim is to try to establish good working relationships with everyone, whatever their rank or position might be.

5. **Find out what working standards are required as the 'norm'.** This can involve completion dates, quality of work standards and all liaison/communication requirements. This is part of your investigations upon 'what is defined as high working standards'. Knowing this gives you a target you should aim for, and possibly exceed. This also includes getting to know the employer's working <u>policies</u>, e.g. standing orders, financial rules,

discipline/grievance procedures and general conditions of employment.

6. **Avoid criticising other employees.** This, however, must be qualified by two conditions. Firstly, by avoiding criticising others for clearly minor transgressions, you improve your relations with others, particularly where you can be seen to be understanding and non-judgemental, when things go wrong. However, in the second scenario, where the particular case is much more serious and which clearly affects the success of work, involves (verifiable) dishonesty, offensive/threatening behaviour, or is <u>clearly</u> contrary to the employer's policies and interests, <u>you have a duty</u> to your employer to take action. First step <u>must</u> be a confidential meeting with your supervisor with a request for advice. Be mindful of the possible presence of 'personal relations' or your 'informal' organisational chart. If you need to take direct action yourself, it <u>must</u> be on the basis of prior consultation and advice from a more senior (trusted) colleague, or any 'mentor' you may have obtained.

7. **Work extra hours during the first few months by arriving early and/or working late (without expectation of reward).** If you are questioned about this, your answer might be that 'in any new job, there is often a need to clock up extra time to more quickly familiarise yourself with new working procedures, company policies and any work which needs more time by a <u>new</u> employee, than for an experienced employee'. The purpose is not to directly impress other people, but to meet all working requirements as soon as possible. Your reliability and integrity will be noted anyway.

8. **Help others where you can, again with no expectation of reward.** This is part of establishing good relations with working colleagues as in 4 above. You may during conversations with others identify

areas of joint interest, or other people's difficulties in their own work, of which you have past experience or knowledge. <u>If you are sure that you can help in some way,</u> give any advice or helpful information that you can. Be careful about actually doing their work. It can improve relations with others, but it can also be viewed as spending time not carrying out your own work. Consider this carefully. Giving suggestions and advice is the safest, so long as you are absolutely sure this will help. Also, compliment others, whenever you think this is justified. Either because their work quality or their occupational skills is of a high standard, or an aspect of their personality is commendable. (It always helps your 'street cred', as the younger members of my family would say!)

9. **Be honest and open on all matters where <u>verifiable information is available</u>, even if this information may be regarded as 'inconvenient'.** Sometimes, you may be asked a question about another person or a particular situation where you know the answer, but you are concerned about the consequences of giving the answer. Provided your answers are verifiably correct and it is an important issue, you need to consider how best to answer, and to whom. If, however, you are not sure about your response, or you simply are not completely sure, say so. But remember, in your mind, the question you were asked, since it may provide 'guidance' for the future! Again, your immediate supervisor comes first, perhaps in confidence, but nevertheless formally. If the matter is **very** serious, you might give your report in writing, but if you do, make <u>damn</u> sure what you write is <u>absolutely accurate</u>, provides the source of your knowledge, and why it affects the employer's interests adversely. For reasons of maintaining your own reputation, you might also add your own 'regret' at providing the information, emphasising that the <u>employer's</u> interests come first in your mind. Finally,

do consider the consequences, if you <u>avoid</u> giving information which may be later shown that you had, and that the employer's interests <u>were</u> affected.

10. **Look out for ways to improve work WHICH WILL BENFIT YOUR EMPLOYERS BUSINESS.** This can involve cost savings without reducing quality, improved 'production' output (whatever that means in your own specific occupational field), and would be popular with your employer's 'clients' (whether commercial or in the public service). Consider, carefully, whether your ideas might create new problems which reduces the 'benefit' aspect. Clearly, this will normally involve your particular area of responsibility, but it can also involve associated activities which you need to coordinate with. You will appreciate that in this scenario, you must avoid 'treading on other people's toes' and adversely affecting good work relationships. It could do your reputation in your new job, much harm, if what you propose is unworkable and proves to be none beneficial. In the first case (your OWN work), you can put forward ideas to your supervisor, which give benefit and does not cause problems to others. In the second case (where someone else is affected), if, again, you are sure of the benefits, you need to discuss it openly with the person(s) involved and if they agree with your suggestions, put them forward as a joint proposal. Again, keep 'the boss' advised and take their directions.

11. **Recognise those in the organisation who have the best, respected reputation.** As well as your own immediate supervisor and those above, you (yourself) need to be recognised by them in the same light. You need them to look on you as working to high standards, have ambitions for both yourself and the employer generally. Express your own appreciation, regularly and openly to others who help and advise

you. If the employer operates any system like 'best employee of the month awards', <u>go for that too</u>.

12. **Fully understand what the 'corporate' objectives are for your employer and know how your own work fits into these aims.** You will know that these mean such things as increased sales/services, reduced costs, production turnover, 'beating' or 'equalling' whoever the competition is, meeting perceived public needs and increased market share. Having this information will enable you to recognise areas in your own work which makes a contribution to achieving those 'corporate' objectives, and help to further enhance your own reputation.

13. **Do not be drawn into 'workplace politics'.** This can be a serious risk to your future success if you become associated with employee groups known for their negative attitudes towards others or to the organisation generally. This is sometimes a difficult problem. On the one hand, you want to be seen as 'friendly' to all, but in some instances, being 'friendly' with the 'wrong' people can influence reputation even when you are doing a good job. Advice from your supervisor is needed first and perhaps your 'mentor'. In **all** relationships there is an ideal 'distance' between various associates. 'Arm's length' or 'close relationships' are the two extremes. Take advice, and determine, for yourself, the relationship 'distance' with others, which do you least harm and increase your reputation and standing. This applies to occupations in both the commercial and the public Sector (see rule 18).

14. **Do not engage in any 'special' relationships.** In most employment situations, we make new acquaintances. This can be related to work activities, mutual (outside) interests/activities, or simply 'friendships'. In some cases, however, these may be seen, by some, to be excessively strong, affecting your own work interest, and responsibilities. If you

suspect that this is affecting yourself, you must, again, establish the right 'distance' between yourself and anyone you are seen to be spending time with. Your first loyalty is to those who pay your salary/wages and have some influence upon your future. If someone is becoming somewhat too attentive to you, you must deal with it in a positive constructive way, without offending anyone. If the difficulty persists, confer with your supervisor, in confidence, and take any advice they can give.

15. **In your own, confidential 'redeployment file', update your records, adding comments as appropriate, and provisionally identify any 'next step' in your own career progression.** Clearly, you should aim to stay with your new employer for—say—a minimum of three years. But do not rely on your own memory to recall important events at that time. You are learning new experiences which may well help you on the next 'rung' of the ladder. Forward planning and accurate records are very important.

16. **Be alert to any activities which you strongly feel are very questionable.** Sadly, in both commercial organisations and the public services, activities take place which are actually contrary to the law, contrary to the employer's interests and policies, and dangerous. Once again, the advice is similar to other situations. Firstly check, carefully, the information you have concerning the particular matter, what you have seen yourself, and the source of any other relevant information. Confirm, as far as you can, that the particular activity, if verified, **is** contrary to established rules. Then, speak, in confidence, to your supervisor or mentor. Keep your own notes in a secure place. Take advice and comply with it. If the activities continue, keep your records up to date. Then, after a reasonable period, if the activities persist, make a confidential written report,

emphasising it is based upon your own knowledge, and your interpretation of the rules. Finally (I have to say), watch your back, very carefully and do nothing more, except your own job.

17. **Take up any opportunities to enhance your professional/technical occupational knowledge.** There are a number of ways to do this. You can attend study courses relevant to your own occupation, enrol in any 'in house' training events, correspondence courses, and your own research from technical/professional publications. You can become an active member of an occupational institute and take part in their programme of talks and meetings, or take a relevant 'open university' course. Try to use your new job as a route to extend the 'training education/qualifications' section in your CV. Keep your supervisor advised and consult/inform at regular intervals. It may even be possible for the employer to support you in this 'extra curriculum' work, if it can be shown to give benefit to the ambitions and objectives of the employer.

18. **Demonstrate your loyalty to the employer, by keeping an eye on the 'opposition'.** This is more appropriate in the commercial fields, of course, and if you see any new developments by competing organisations, or extensions of activity, which might have escaped the attention of 'corporate' levels of your own employer, mention and report it providing the source of the information. In the case of public sector organisations, the emphasis is different, but nonetheless important. Here, there are many different ways and levels of providing various services. There are many publications directly relevant to specific service provisions. They give articles upon what other public bodies are doing and how. If you become a member of a relevant occupational institute, additional information is available at meetings, along the same lines as with publications. By comparing

what they do, to what your own employer does, whatever variations you identify in terms of productivity, costs and types of services provided, can inspire ideas for improvements, which could be provided by your own (public) employer.

19. **Look for any opportunity to 'sell' or advertise the work of your employer.** This does not mean placing your own advertisements selling the services of your employer! It might mean—for example—keeping an eye on potential new marketing sites where there is, presently, no similar service within the immediate vicinity. It might mean extending the employers own website by adding specialised news events upon your own occupational area. It might mean enabling and helping your supervisor to increase positive media exposure for the directors of the organisation. Every occupational employment area is the subject of specialised media activity and publications. Look at what other employers are doing in these areas and if appropriate, replicate and improve their activities to benefit your own organisation.

20. **Take any available opportunity to enhance the reputation of your immediate supervisor.** This might mean that if you have (yourself) any brilliant new way to improve services, cut costs, do better than the 'opposition', and you are convinced of its benefits to your employing organisation, explain it to your supervisor, try to get the idea adopted, and allow your supervisor to present the idea AND to take credit for it. After all, your supervisor has taken a little risk for presenting it in his own name and the risk of the idea failing in some way. If this works, you will, again, enhance your own reputation and that of your supervisor, and this should ensure future support in your own occupational development in the future.

'To Infinity and Beyond' (Preparedness for <u>Future</u> Changes)

<u>'To infinity and beyond!'</u> (I love ANY kind of science fiction!)

So, you have gone through all the steps on your route to a better life and you are now in a happier more suitable occupation to you interests and talents. You are achieving a good personal reputation. **Well done, again!** Is this the end of the story? Well, not quite. One final task, easily defined and carried out, must be done. It can be defined very simply. <u>You do not want to have to travel this route again.</u> Agreed? So a few **final** (really!) suggestions.

- Use all your past experience to remain alert to future change. Remember; <u>'change **remains** an inevitability'</u> even for successful people.
- Retain your own 'occupational development' file and keep it up to date with notes and comments. Keep a weather eye open for signs of change. At the time of writing this book, the damage to the environment by plastics has finally been recognised. Change HAS to come. People in the plastics business may now be vulnerable to unemployment. <u>However,</u> those people who have effective proposals to <u>rectify</u> this serious problem are not vulnerable. They will be increasingly successful.
- In your file, open up a new section which considers, even at this time, how you will deal with any future 'occupational' risk. Another change in occupational <u>type</u>? Same occupation, but at a higher level? Going to a different employer? Going self-employed in a new developing business, e.g. collapsible pre-packed furniture? (Sorry, that's already been done!)

As a former boy scout, I commend to you their simple motto, 'Be prepared'.

Conclusion

If all the forgoing sections could be condensed into 7 key points, to my own mind, they would be as follows:

- Hard work and better self-confidence.
- Benefits you provide—to the employer.
- Personal reputation and contribution.
- Reliability and honesty.
- Occupational self-development in your new job.
- Accurate, verifiable and relevant information.
- Future personal planning.

I will conclude by expressing the hope that, even if this book's contents are not all those you need in your own particular case, some parts at least, will be relevant and helpful and that the result is a happier and more fulfilling life. **I wish you every success in your future occupations and in your life generally!**

Appendix One

80 Sample Interview Questions

Example Questions Which Might Be Asked During the Interview

It is impossible to anticipate all the questions likely to be asked at any interview. The following 80 questions are, intentionally, randomly listed for practice purposes. You can go through them picking out, say, any 10 for each practice only. The purpose of the exercise is to give you experience at extracting information from your memory fairly rapidly to answer the question, whether this is information which you have carefully prepared for, or other information which you did not think you would need. You will appreciate that the questions are 'open', general questions which cannot be answered simply with a 'yes' or 'no'. The intention is to make you talk about a variety of subject areas. Some of the questions are, again, intentionally, controversial—even discriminating. This is because, with the exception of 'trained interviewers' who will ask 'proper' questions, you may also be interviewed by others who are not so able. This might be so, but you must still be ready to respond to them in a measured, relevant, and calm manner.

1) When would you be able to start if you were offered the post? Could you start earlier?
2) What activities would you like to take up when you retire?

3) Hello, Mr Richardson has been called away to an urgent meeting. I am his assistant and I am willing to interview you. Are you happy with this?

4) Which do you prefer? To work on your own or in a team, and why?

5) If you had a free-hand, what would you change in your current job, and why?

6) If we offered you this job, how long would you like to remain in it and why?

7) Forgive me, but you seem to be a little nervous/flustered/overweight?

8) Which do you think is more important, salary or job satisfaction? Why?

9) What was the most complex system/equipment that you operated during the last year? How did you cope?

10) What activity gave you the least fulfilment and the most enjoyment at school, and in your first employment?

11) What training would you personally need if you were appointed?

12) You seem somewhat under-qualified for this post. What do you feel about that?

13) If you could change your current job, how would you do it, and why?

14) 'Sell' yourself to me, in one minute.

15) Which personal qualities do you think are important in this job?

16) Your handwriting suggests that you may be irrational from time to time. How would you respond to that observation?

17) Have you discussed your career with anyone during the last year? If so, what conclusion did you arrive at?

18) What activities at school, and during your first employment gave you most fulfilment and enjoyment?

19) Everyone experiences some stress and problems at work. What was your most recent experience of this? How did you manage it?

20) How do you think this job might develop?

21) Describe your ideal supervisor.

22) What television programmes do you watch? Why do you like them?

23) What developments does your present company have for the future?

24) If you were offered the post at a lower salary, would you consider it?

25) How would your last employer describe your talents and shortcomings?

26) As a supervisor, what work qualities would you look for from your staff?

27) How do you relate to people whom you don't particularly like?

28) If you could go back to the start of your career, what would you change? If so, what to and, why?

29) Do you plan your working day? If so, how?

30) Do you do any charity work? If so, what?

31) What improvements would you like to achieve in the job immediately, if you were appointed?

32) What are your particular reasons for seeking another job from the one you now have?

33) Have you had any health problems during the last three years? If so, what were they?

34) What talents do you think you have, which other candidates do not have?

35) What do you think is important when coming to decisions?

36) Why did you leave ABC company (past employer)? And/or why do you want to leave your present job?

37) How would you start work, if we appointed you?

38) Are you going to take any future training courses? If so, what subjects?

39) Has your current/past supervisor got any shortcomings?

40) What kind of vacancy would be ideal for your talents, experience and qualifications?

41) How would you describe your health?

42) Are you worried about any aspect of the job?
43) What do you think you have learnt from your current/past job?
44) How would you deal with a case of persistent bad timekeeping by a subordinate? How would you deal with misconduct or poor working standards?
45) What have you found out about our company?
46) What physical exercise do you take? How often?
47) Do you prefer to be a small fish in a big pond or a big fish in a small pond?
48) How much do you miss work whilst you are on vacation?
49) What recent news item attracted your particular interest and why?
50) Have your qualifications helped in your career? If so, how and to what extent?
51) Describe a recent task where you think you failed, and say why.
52) Sum up your strengths and your weaknesses.
53) Do you drink or smoke?
54) What mistakes do you think you have made during the last five years?
55) What are your feelings about travelling or being away from home for long periods with your job?
56) What newspapers and periodicals do you read at the moment? And why?
57) What other jobs have you applied for?
58) Describe a task that you have recently carried out, which gave you a real satisfaction and state why.
59) What are you particularly good at?
60) What are your views about equal opportunities?
61) Do you set objectives for yourself at work and/or in your personal life?
62) Can you describe the ideal supervisor/manager?
63) What income levels are you anticipating?
64) Where would you like to be in five years' time?
65) In a nutshell, why should we give you this appointment?

66) Why do you want to leave your current job? Your response will be treated entirely in confidence.
67) How long do you think it is reasonable for someone to stay in one job?
68) What do you feel are the company's major strengths? What are their weaknesses?
69) If you suspected someone of theft or other forms of unacceptable behaviour, how would you deal with it?
70) What is your vision of success (for yourself)?
71) Is there any particular work in this vacancy where you feel your experience/training is inadequate?
72) How would you handle an argument with your supervisor?
73) What problems do you think our company is encountering at the moment?
74) If we appointed you, what would be your most important priority?
75) Do you have a family? What kind of demands do they make on you?
76) Have you any attributes which you feel have been wasted?
77) Do you take work home? Do you think this is a good thing or not, and why?
78) Have you been prosecuted for any form of unlawful activity during the last five years?
79) Who did you vote for in the last general election and what were your reasons for doing so?
80) How would you react if it became necessary to alter your job/work six months after appointment?

Appendix Two
Alphabetical List of Occupations

The following listing is (regretfully) long and quite detailed. The intention for providing this information is to give an opportunity for you to read through the list and perhaps, simply, to tick, say, 5/6 occupations which, either from your past experience or your intuition, seem to be interesting. Other occupations you might notice may come to mind, which you have not previously thought of, needing additional research on the web. I hope this exercise might prove useful.

A

Abattoir worker
Accommodation warden
Accounting technician
Accounts clerk
Actor
Actuary
Acupuncturist
Administration
Advertising
Aeronautical engineer
Agricultural contractor
Agricultural scientist
Agricultural tester and inspector
Air cabin crew
Air conditioning
Aircraft maintenance

Air Force: men and women
Air hostess/steward
Airport jobs
Air traffic controller
Ambulance staff
Ancient buildings work
Animal nurse
Animal technician
Animals: work with
Antiques dealer/restorer
Arboriculturalist
Archaeology
Architect
Archivist
Art exhibition organiser
Art gallery work
Art teacher
Art therapist
Arts administrator
Assembler (electronics)
Astrologer
Astrophysicist
Auctioneer
Audiologist
Audio typist
Audio-visual technician
Au pair
Auto electrician
Automobile repairers

B

Baker
Ballet dancer
Ballroom dance teacher
Bank staff
Barrister's clerk
Bar staff
Beautician

Beauty therapist
Beauty consultant
Bee keeper
Betting and gaming
Bilingual secretary
Biology/biologist
Biomedical engineer
Birds: work with
Blacksmith
Boat builder
Bookbinder (machine)
Book seller
Brewing
Bricklayer
British Telecom staff
Broadcaster (technical)
Building
Building manager
Building technician
Building services
Building societies staff
Building surveyor
Bursar
Bus driver/conductor
Business machine repairer
Business manager
Butcher
Butler
Buyer (retail)
Buyer (industry)

C

Camera work (films)
Camera work (television)
Canine beautician
Canteen assistant
Cardiologist
Care assistant (children)

Clerical work – general
Clerk of Court
Customs work
Cloakroom attendant
Clothes packer
Clothing industry
Coach driver
Coach (sport)
Coal miner
Commercial artist
Commodity broker
Communications engineer
Community nurse
Community work
Company secretary
Composer
Computer careers
Computer engineer
Computer operator
Computer programmer
Confectioner
Conference organiser
Conservation (historical)
Conservation (nature)
Construction manager
Construction plant operator
Consumer advice
Consumer protection
Cook – general
Cook housekeeper
Copy typist
Copy writer (advertising)
Costumes work
Counter service assistant
Countryside manager
Craftsperson – designer
Crane driver

Credit controller/manager
Credit trader

D

Dairy industry
Dancer/dance teacher
Data preparation officer
Deckhand – Merchant Navy
Decorating (cakes etc.)
Decorator (ceramics)
Decorator (interior)
Delivery work
Demolition work
Dental careers
Dental hygienist/therapist
Dental surgery assistant
Dental technician
Derrick man/woman
Desk top publishing
Detective (private)
Dietitian
Disabled people: jobs with
Display work (shops)
Distribution industry
District nurse
Diver
Dogs: work with
Domestic appliance repairer
Domestic worker – cleaning
Domestic worker –general
Drama
Draftsman
Dress designers
Dresser (theatre)
Dress maker
Driller – oil
Driving instructor
Driving – rail

Driving – road
Dry cleaning

E

Editor
Electrical engineer
Electrical installation
Electrician
Electronics work
Embalmer
Embroidery
Emergency services
Employment agency work
Energy supply/technology
Engineering – agricultural
Engineering – automobile
Engineering – biomedical
Engineering – building services
Engineering – chemical
Engineering – communications
Engineering – computer
Engineering – control
Engineering – design
Engineering – electrical
Engineering – electronic
Engineering – gas
Engineering – heating
Engineering – highways
Engineering – horticultural
Engineering – illuminating/lighting
Engineering – manufacturing systems
Engineering – marine
Engineering – mechanical
Engineering – mining
Engineering – production
Engineering – radio and TV repairs
Engineering – refrigeration
Engineering – shipbuilding

Engineering – structural
Engineering – communications
Engineering – telephone
Engineering – television
Engineering – ventilating
Entertainer
Entertainments – administration
Environmental health
Estate agent
Estate manager
Executive officer
Executive – legal
Exhibition designer
Exhibition organiser
Exporter

F

Factory inspector
Factory worker
Farming
Farming – small-scale
Farm manager
Farm secretary
Farm worker
Fashion buyer
Fashion designer
Fashion manufacture
Fashion model
Fast food worker
Felt roofer
Filing clerk
Film work
Financial work
Fire fighter
Fish farmer
Fishing
Fishmonger
Flight engineer

Flight planner
Florist
Flower grower
Forces. Navy, Army, Air force.
Food industry – production
Food preparation
Food service
Forensic scientist
Forestry
Fork lift truck driver
Fostering
Foundry worker
Freight forwarder
Fruit grower
Fuel technologist
Funeral director
Furnace work
Furniture designer/maker
Furniture removals

G

Gamekeeper
Garage work
Garden centres
Gardener
Gas engineer
Genetics
Geography
Geology/geophysics
Glass technologist
Glazier
Goldsmith
Graphic art/design
Graphologist
Groom
Groundsman/woman
Guide – historic buildings

Guide – tourist
Gun making

H

Hairdresser
Handicapped people: jobs with
Hat making
Health/safety inspector
Health administration
Health education officer
Health service work
Health visitor
Heating and ventilation
Heavy goods vehicle driver
Heavy plant operator
Herbal medicine
HGV driver
History/historical work
Holiday camp work
Home carer
Home help
Homeopath
Horse racing
Horses: work with
Horticulture
Hospices: work in
Hospital administrator
Hospital work
Hospital porter
Hotel and catering work
Hotel manager
Hotel porter
Hotel receptionist
Housekeeper (domestic)
Housekeeper (hotel)
Housekeeper (institutional)
Houseparent
Housing manager

Hydrographic surveyor

I

Illumination engineer
Illustrator
Immigration officer
Importer
income tax inspector
Industrial designer
Industrial manager
Industrial relations (personnel)
Industrial relations (trade unions)
Industrial safety
Industrial trainer
Information officer
Insurance
Interior decorator
Interior designer
Interpreter
Investment analyst

J

Jewellery – retail
Jewellery – designer
Jockey
Joiner
Journalist
Justice's clerk
Justice's clerk's assistant

K

Keeper – museum
Keeper – zoo
Keep fit instructor
Kennel worker
Kitchen fitting

Kitchen worker

Knitwear designer
Knitwear manufacture

L

Laboratory work
Labourer – building
Labourer – factory
Landscape gardener
Languages
Laundry work
Leather industry
Legal executive
Legal profession: work in
Legal secretary
Leisure manager
Libraries: work in
Library assistant
Licensed trade
Lighting engineer
Lighting – theatrical etc.
Linguist
Livestock
Locksmith
Lorry driver
Loss adjuster – insurance

M

Mental illness nurse
Merchandising manager
Machinist – servicing
Machinist – woodworking
Maintenance work – cars
Maintenance work – domestic
Maintenance work – industrial
Maintenance work – office machines

Make-up work – beautician
Make-up work – television
Management
Manager – hotels
Manager – housing
Manager – retail
Manufacturing systems engineering
Marine biologist
Marine engineer
Marines
Market gardener
Marketing
Market research
Materials scientist
Matron – school
Mechanic – vehicles
Mechanical engineer
Media planner – advertising
Media: working in
Medical herbalist
Medical illustrator
Medical jobs and careers
Medical laboratory staff
Medical photographer
Medical physics
Medical profession
Medical records work
Medical sales representative
Medical secretary
Medical social worker
Mental handicap nurse
Mental handicap teacher
Mental health work
Merchant banker
Merchant Navy – officers
Merchant Navy – ratings
Messenger
Metallurgy

Meteorology
Microbiology
Mid Wife
Millinery
Minerals surveyor
Mining engineer
Mining geologist
Minister of religion
Mobility instructor
Modeller (ceramics)
Model (fashion etc.)
Model maker – general
Model maker – museum
Mothers help
Motorcycle maintenance
Motorcycle messenger
Motor mechanic
Municipal engineer
Museum staff
Musical instruments technology
Musician
Music therapist

N

Nanny
Nature conservation
Nature reserve warden
Naturopath
Navy – Merchant (officers)
Navy – Merchant (ratings)
Needlework
Newspaper work
Nurse
Nurse: dental
Nurse: mentally handicapped
Nurse: mentally ill
Nurse: Registered
Nurse: school

Nurse: veterinary
Nurseries – plant
Nursery nurse
Nursery school teacher
Nursing auxiliary

O

Occupational health nurse
Occupational hygienist
Occupational psychologist
Occupational therapist
Oceanography
Office administration
Office cleaning
Office work – general
Oil technologist
Oil refinery work
Operational research
Optical technician
Optician
Ordnance survey
Organic farming
Organisation and methods
Orthoptist
Osteopath
Overseas work – permanent
Overseas work – temporary
Overseas work – voluntary

P

Porter – railway
Port worker
Packaging designer
Packaging technologist
Painter and decorator
Paint technologist
Paper mill work

Paper technology
Paramedical work
Parks and gardens work
Parts work (motor)
Party political agent
Passenger service assistants
Patents work
Pattern maker (foundries)
Pensions work
Personal secretary
Personnel work
Pest controller
Pet shop work
Petrol station attendant
Pharmaceuticals
Pharmacology
Photography – general
Photography – medical
Photography – police
Photography – press
Physical education
Physics
Physiological measurement
Physiology
Physiotherapist assistant
Piano tuner
Picture restorer
Planner – town/country
Plant mechanic (construction)
Plasterer
Plastics industry
Play leader
Plumber
Police civilian work
Police work
Polymer technologist
Porter
Porter – hospital

Porter – hotel
Postman/woman
Post Office work
Pottery designer
Pottery industry worker
Poultry farmer
Press photographer
Printing
Prison service
Probation officer
Process/production worker
Producer – films
Producer – TV and radio
Producer – theatre
Production engineer
Production line work
Production management
Professional musician
Programmer – computer
Psychiatric nurse
Psychiatric social worker
Psychiatrist
Psychologist
Publican
Public analyst
Public health
Public relations officer
Publishing
Purser – passenger liners

Q

Quality assurance
Quality control laboratory work
Quantity surveyor
Quarrying

R

Racing – cars
Racing – horses
Radiographer
Radiologist
Radio and TV – producing
Radio and TV – technical
Radio and TV – servicing
Radio officer – Merchant Navy
Radio telephone operator
Radiotherapist
Railways work
Ranger
Rating and valuation
Receptionist – general
Receptionist – hotels
Receptionist – medical
Recording studio work
Recreation manager
Refrigeration
Refuse collector
Registrar
Religion
Reporter
Researcher – broadcasting
Research officer – Civil Service
Residential care – children
Residential care – elderly
Restaurant manager
Retail – buyer
Retailing
Retail manager
Riding instructor
Road maintenance
Road safety officer
Road transport
Roofer
Room attendant (hotel)

RSPCA inspector
Rural crafts
Rural practice surveying

S

Saddler
Safety officer
Sales assistant
Sales demonstrator
Sales representative
Sports teacher
Sports therapist
Scaffolder
Scenes of crime officer
School teacher
Schools – non-teaching jobs
Sculptor
Sea fishing
Secretary
Security officer
Selling – representative
Selling – sales assistant
Servicing – cars
Servicing – domestic
Servicing – industrial
Servicing – office machines
Set designer
Sewing machinist
Sheet metal work
Shelf filler (shops)
Shepherd
Ship broker
Ship builder
Shoe repairer
Shop fitting
Shop keeping – self-employed
Shop assistant
Shop work

Shorthand typist
Show business
Sign writer
Silversmith
Singer
Slaughterhouse worker
Spray painter
Social worker
Sociologist
Soft furnishings
Software designer/engineer
Solicitor
Sound recordist
Speech therapist
Sponsorships
Sport (related careers)
Sports centre staff
Sports coach
Stable worker
Stage hand
Stage manager
Statistician
Steeplejack
Sterile supplies worker
Stewardess – airline
Stewardess – ships
Stockbroker
Stockman/woman
Stone mason
Storekeeper
Street cleaner
Structural engineer
Studio manager
Stunt artist
Surgeon
Surgical appliance fitter
Surveyor

Swimming pool attendant
Systems analyst

T

Tailor
Tax inspector
Taxi driver
Taxidermist
Teacher
Technical assistant (broadcasting)
Technical illustrator
Technical sales/service
Technical writer
Telecommunications
Telephone engineer
Telephonist
Telephone sales staff
Television broadcaster
Television engineer
Television servicing
Tennis player
Theatre – acting
Theatre – backstage work
Thermal insulator
Three-dimensional design
Tiler
Timber felling/growing
Timber technology/trade
Tour guide
Tourism
Tour operator
Town/country planner
Tractor driver
Trade union work
Trading standard work
Traffic scheduler
Traffic warden
Train driver

Trainer
Translator
Transport escort
Transport manager
Transport – rail
Transport – road
Travel agency work
Travel – jobs involving
TV broadcasting
TV engineering
TV servicing
Typist
Tyre fitter

U

Undertaker
Underwriter – insurance
Unorthodox medicine
Upholsterer
Usher – court

V

Valuer
Van driver
Vehicle body work
Vehicle designer
Vehicle repairer
Vending machine attendant
Ventilation engineer
Veterinary nurse
Vending machine attendant
Ventilation engineer
Veterinary nurse
Video work
Voluntary work – overseas
Voluntary work – UK

W

Wages clerk
Waiter/waitress
Warden – accommodation
Warden – institutional
Warden – conservation
Ward orderly
Wardrobe – theatre
Warehouse worker
Watch repairer
Water bailiff
Water industry
Weather forecasting
Weights and measures
Welder
Welfare assistant – school
Welfare work
Wholesaling
Window cleaner
Window dresser
Wood working
Word processor operator
Working from home
Work study
Writing
Writing – journalism
Writing – technical
Wrought iron work

Y

Yacht builder
Youth training
Youth worker

Z

Zoology
Zoos: work in

The End